Barbara Ellis, Editor

Frances Tenenbaum, Series Editor

HOUGHTON MIFFLIN COMPANY
Boston • New York 1997

Safe & Easy Lawn Care

THE COMPLETE GUIDE TO ORGANIC, LOW-MAINTENANCE LAWNS

For information about permission to reproduce selections from this book,
write to Permissions, Houghton Mifflin Company, 215 Park Avenue South,
New York, New York 10003.

For information about this and other Houghton Mifflin trade
and reference books and multimedia products, visit The Bookstore at
Houghton Mifflin on the World Wide Web at http://www.hmco.com/trade/.

Taylor's Guide is a registered trademark of Houghton Mifflin Company.

Library of Congress Cataloging-in-Publication Data

Safe and easy lawn care / Barbara Ellis, editor.
      p. cm. — (Taylor's weekend gardening guides)
    Includes index.
    ISBN 0-395-81369-7
    1. Lawns. I. Ellis, Barbara W. II. Series.
  SB433.S25 1997
    635.9'647 — dc20   97-15899

Printed in the United States of America.

RMT 10 9 8 7 6 5 4 3 2 1

Book design by Deborah Fillion
Cover photograph © by HOM Photography

CONTENTS

INTRODUCTION 1

CHAPTER 1 — PLANNING A LOW-MAINTENANCE LAWN 3
How Much Lawn Do You Need? 4
Design Considerations 4
Plan Ahead for Easier Care 12
Consider Alternatives to Lawn Grass 18
Meadows and Prairies 22

CHAPTER 2 — PLANTING A HEALTHY LAWN 25
Choosing the Best Grass 25
A Guide to Warm-Season Grasses 29
A Guide to Cool-Season Grasses 32
Preparing the Soil 33
Planting Options 39
Seeding a Lawn 40
Laying Sod 42
Planting Plugs and Sprigs 44

CHAPTER 3 — CARING FOR YOUR LAWN 47
Mowing 47
Watering 50
Fertilizing 53
Edging and Trimming 57

CHAPTER 4 — RENOVATING A LAWN 61
What's the Problem? 62
Reducing Maintenance 64
Dealing with Thatch 69
Aerating and Top-Dressing 71
Overseeding 72
Reseeding and Resodding 73
Removing an Old Lawn 76

CHAPTER 5 — COPING WITH PESTS, DISEASES, AND WEEDS 79
A Guide to Lawn Pests 81
Managing Lawn Diseases 90
A Guide to Common Lawn Diseases 92
Controlling Weeds 95

HARDINESS ZONE MAP 115
CREDITS 116
INDEX 117

Homeowners everywhere are changing the way they look at their lawns. To be sure, a lush, green carpet is still the ideal, but today, everyone wants a lawn that looks great with a minimum of care and attention. This book provides complete information on planning and planting an attractive lawn that is easy to care for — plus directions for renovating and reducing maintenance on existing, problem-plagued lawns. In addition to basic, step-by-step directions for preparing the soil, sowing seed, and planting sod, it features safe, all-organic controls for common pests, diseases, and weeds. Ideas for designing an effective lawn and reducing maintenance chores like edging and trimming make an easy-care lawn a reality.

Mass plantings of ornamental grasses are drought-tolerant and easy to care for. Consider combining them with conventional lawns to reduce the area that you must mow and water regularly.

Chapter 1:
Planning a Low-Maintenance Lawn

Even gardeners who plan flower beds and borders with meticulous detail are apt to overlook planning altogether when they plant a lawn. Most homeowners simply use the lawn to fill up the space between the other features in a yard — flower gardens, shrub borders, paths, patios, utility areas, and so forth. That's too bad, because a well-planned lawn can be a striking feature in a design. In a small courtyard garden a simple oval of well-kept grass surrounded by shrubs and perennials can add an air of cool, elegant formality. Wide, smooth paths of grass in a larger yard make strolling among flower beds exciting and pleasurable.

Taking time to plan where you plant a lawn can help you avoid maintenance headaches and recurring problems, too. Planning beds of ground covers on steep sites will eliminate sweaty sessions with the lawn mower week after week, and year after year. And planning how you will deal with areas where grass won't grow

A small lawn with a simple, formal shape adds elegance to this tiny garden and makes it seem larger. The smooth texture of the grass contrasts with the flowers and shrubs in the beds that surround it.

well, such as low, marshy spots, will help you avoid problems with weak, unhealthy turf that repeatedly needs replacing.

Whether you are planning a new lawn or looking for ways to make an existing lawn more effective and efficient, you'll find a wealth of ideas in this chapter. It's a good idea to start by making a rough sketch of your yard. Draw in your house, outbuildings like sheds or garages, and any existing plantings like flower beds, vegetable gardens, trees, and shrubs. Then take a walk around your yard and identify spots where lawn grass might be hard to care for or where it might not thrive. Make a note of slopes, wet spots, areas with heavy traffic, and so forth. Then use the photographs and text in this chapter to look for solutions that work for you.

HOW MUCH LAWN DO YOU NEED?

Lawns occupy such a large proportion of most lots, and tending them can take so much time and effort, it's worth thinking carefully about how much lawn you need and what you need it for. Your lawn's size depends on several factors, not the least of which is your budget. If you're establishing a new lawn, you'll soon learn that laying several thousand square feet of sod can be a pricey proposition; you may opt for a smaller lawn bordered by ground cover or natural areas. The size of your family also affects this decision. Children enjoy playing on spacious lawns, but couples and single adults often find small lawns more appealing. Don't forget that the amount of maintenance is directly proportional to the amount of grass. The larger your lawn, the more time you'll spend mowing, fertilizing, raking, and watering.

DESIGN CONSIDERATIONS

From a design standpoint, the lawn's most important function is to serve as a unifier. It links a garden's major elements, such as trees, shrubs, flower borders, walks, and pools. It's also a transporter, both visually and physically, taking you from one area of the property to another. And it can enhance the other plantings by establishing interesting textural and color contrasts. You can juxtapose, for example, the rigid formality of a closely cropped lawn with a naturalistic

A well-designed lawn can be a strong, unifying element in a landscape design. This lawn features sweeping curves that link the side and backyards visually and make it easy to move from one part of the yard to another.

Bulbs in the Lawn

Bulbs spread throughout a lawn are a lovely sight in spring *(below),* but they do pose a dilemma for lawn care. Mowing the lawn after the bulbs flower cuts down the foliage, preventing the bulbs from making food for next year's display. In areas planted with naturalized bulbs, you must be willing to leave the grass unmowed until the bulb foliage turns yellow. This could be any time from June to August, depending on where you live. By

that time, you'll have a luxuriant crop of grass *(below),* which you may need to use a string trimmer to cut to a manageable height before mowing. Another option is to only naturalize small bulbs, like crocuses, and mow high, over the foliage. To plant bulbs in a lawn, skim off areas of sod, dig to the required depth, plant, and then replace the sod. Or use a bulb planter and dig individual holes for bulbs.

The shape of a lawn can become a strong, unifying element in a garden design. The smooth expanse of this free-form lawn creates a stark contrast with the riotous beds that surround it. The gently curving shape provides welcome visual relief and introduces movement and flow into the design.

woodland planting of dogwoods, native azaleas, and wildflowers. Or you can play off the smooth green surface of a lawn and contrast it with plantings of mixed ground covers like ajuga, junipers, and English ivy.

Shape is something most people don't connect with a lawn. In fact, in many neighborhoods, lawns are essentially shapeless, blending into one another in a continuous strip of green down one side of the street. This is unfortunate, for a well-defined lawn can be a dynamic part of your overall design. A central rectangle or oval of lawn surrounded by mixed plantings of shrubs and perennials will make a small garden appear larger. To define the shape of your lawn in a neighborhood where lawns run into one another, try placing planting beds between it and the adjacent lawns. Another way to emphasize the shape of your lawn is to edge it with brick.

Keep topography and architecture in mind when deciding on the shape of your lawn. In small city courtyard gardens, where the ground is flat and the

Stone terraces surround a flat, easy-to-mow space in this yard, which features areas of shade and sun. The shady, sloping sites above the terraces are planted with shade-loving ferns and other perennials for a low-maintenance ground cover.

houses tend to be formal, a rectangular or oval lawn is appropriate. A simple hourglass shape or two offset squares can be effective as well. Simple shapes like rectangles, ovals, or hourglasses also are effective in larger, relatively flat yards. In suburban or rural areas where rolling hills and large shade trees foster a more natural, less restrictive atmosphere, an undulating, curvilinear lawn may be a better choice. A curvilinear lawn is more difficult to design, as curves are harder to work with than straight lines. As a result, people often end up with a series of awkward squiggles snaking their way across the ground instead of pleasant, broadly

Topography helped determine the boundaries of this informal lawn. The lawn gives way to shrubs and trees where the slope begins to fall off and the terrain would be difficult to mow.

Areas of lawn flow like water between island beds in this country garden. The lawn accents the beds and makes it easy to enjoy them from all sides.

This well-designed space combines lawn for children's games with terraced perennial beds that eliminate tough-to-mow slopes and provide gardening space for adults in the household. Crushed stone mulch under the swingset replaces grass, which would be hard to grow because of soil compaction and difficult to trim as well. Shredded bark would provide a softer surface.

sweeping curves. Try using a garden hose to outline the proposed boundary of the lawn. That way, you can eyeball the entire curve and adjust it so that it flows smoothly.

PLAN AHEAD FOR EASIER CARE

A well-thought-out design is more than aesthetic; it also reduces maintenance. If you'd rather spend your weekends sipping lemonade by the pool than raking clippings by the sidewalk, take heed of the following design tips. For more low-maintenance tips, see "Reducing Maintenance" on page 64.

- Minimize the number of sharp corners in the lawn so that you can mow the lawn smoothly instead of constantly stopping and backing up.

- Plan how you will move your mower from your garage or shed to all the areas you need to mow. Continuous, connected spaces are easier to mow than patches of lawn.
- Design grass paths so they are a convenient width to mow. If you have a 3-foot-wide mower, you can easily cut a 5- to 5½-foot-wide path in two passes. Any wider, and you'll probably have to

Don't underestimate the power of even a single strip of lawn. This grass path curves gracefully along mixed beds, creating movement and intrigue in the process. The path leads the eye through the garden, compelling visitors to follow it around the bend to discover what is just out of sight.

Casual grass paths leading around a series of planting beds that fill the entire yard may be the best option for an ardent plant collector.

make an extra pass to cut a 2- or 3-inch-wide strip of grass that you missed.

- Plan on covering high-traffic areas with pavers or decking so you don't have to repeatedly deal with compacted soil and dying grass.
- Leave sufficient space between trees in the lawn so that you can easily mow between them. If possible, design mulched beds around trees and shrubs so you don't have to mow between them at all.
- Place mailboxes, lampposts, and bird feeders in the middle of

Paving stones along a commonly traveled path help direct traffic and eliminate the need to cope with lawn grass struggling to grow in compacted soil.

The cluster of round paving stones on the edge of this lawn not only accents the container-grown garden on the patio, it also solves a potential problem. The pavers provide a pathway off the patio and eliminate problems with soil compaction and unhealthy turf that are characteristic of high-traffic areas.

It's possible to mow steep slopes like this one with ropes and pulleys attached to the lawn mower to haul it up and down, but why would you want to? These junipers would need regular weeding until they filled in, but after that, they need almost no care — just trim off wayward shoots and pull an occasional weed.

planting beds, not the lawn, so that you won't have to mow or edge around them.

• Don't grow grass on steep slopes that are difficult and dangerous to mow. Instead, plant an appropriate, low-maintenance ground cover. For a sunny bank, consider ajuga, thyme, low-growing cotoneasters, or junipers. For shady slopes, try English ivy, pachysandra, liriope, or vinca.

• Don't plant grass in heavy shade — it won't thrive. Mulch the area or plant shade-loving ground covers, perennials, or shrubs instead.

Instead of struggling to grow grass on a shady site with wet soil, this homeowner created a pond and wildflower garden — a much more effective and low-maintenance solution for what could be a troublesome site.

Large areas planted in ground covers like thyme give a lawnlike effect, without all the maintenance a lawn requires.

CONSIDER ALTERNATIVES TO LAWN GRASS

In most cases, grass is an ideal ground cover. It spreads rapidly, knitting the soil in place with thick roots and stolons. It is inexpensive, comparatively free of insects and diseases, and requires little care other than mowing. There are situations, however, in which lawn grass is not the answer for covering the ground. Consider alternatives for spots that are too dry, too wet, or too steep to mow.

In areas of the country where traditional turfgrasses can't survive without heavy irrigation, consider planting a lawn of more drought-tolerant native grasses,

Native grasses are becoming more and more popular in the West as drought-tolerant substitutes for lawns. This is sideoats gramma grass.

Brick edging strips define the edges of this grass path running between perennial borders. The bricks keep lawn grasses from invading the flowers and also make it possible to trim and mow in one pass.

such as buffalograss and blue gramma grass. Both are drought-tolerant warm-season grasses that can get by on less than half the water that other common grasses require. In cooler areas, tall fescue and red fescue are the most drought-tolerant types of grasses.

In any part of the country, cutting down the size of your lawn will help conserve water — and save time spent watering. Consider replacing areas of lawn

In this New Mexico garden, lawn has been replaced entirely by low-maintenance alternatives. Mixed plantings of low-growing perennials and ground covers, including sedums and thymes, create a carpet of color, and brick-paved areas provide spaces for gathering outdoors.

grass with plantings of drought-tolerant ornamental grasses, perennials, shrubs, and other ground covers. Combine them with areas of ground-level decking, mulched areas, or paving stones interplanted with drought-tolerant plants like sedums and thyme. Or, you might do away with grass entirely. Some gardeners in the Southwest have created spectacular home landscapes with just native plants, stone mulch, paths, and bare soil.

Meadows and Prairies

In many parts of the country, gardeners are planting wildflower meadows and prairies to reduce the amount of lawn area they mow and tend. Wildflower meadows and prairies do take much less mowing than lawns, but they are *not* a no-work alternative. Establishing a wildflower meadow or prairie involves more than just throwing a handful of flower seeds on the lawn and watching them burst into bloom. Start by selecting a mix of wildflowers and native grasses that has been developed for your region of the country. Avoid generic mixes developed for the entire country or "instant" meadow mixes, which generally contain mostly annuals. Then plan to prepare the soil so you will be ready to plant at the proper

This strip of wildflowers features yarrows (Achillea spp.), evening primroses (Oenothera spp.), coreopsis, and gaillardia. All are drought-tolerant natives.

time. Once the growth is established, you have to maintain it and mow it regularly, though infrequently, to help encourage the flowers.

The best way to turn a small patch of lawn into meadow or prairie is to start with flower transplants, either homegrown or store-bought. In midsummer, mark out the area you plan to plant, mow it as close as possible, then till it under. Wait two weeks and till shallowly again to kill newly sprouted weeds. Repeat the tilling process two or three more times to control weeds. Then use a bulb planter or a trowel to dig up patches of sod for the plants. Arrange the plants in a random pattern, clumping groups of the same plants together in some areas. Water and then mulch the plants with chopped leaves or other organic mulch — up to but not touching the stems — to control weeds.

For larger areas, seed is the only economical way to go. To seed a meadow, mow as close as possible. Then repeat the tilling process as you would for seed. In Zone 3 and south, plan to be ready to sow one month before the first frost of fall. Or sow in early spring as soon as you can work the soil. Once the soil has been prepared, broadcast seed over the entire area. Then top-dress with a $1/4$-inch layer of topsoil or finely screened compost and water it well.

Weed your new meadow by walking thorough it every few weeks and pulling up unwanted plants. Cut it annually in winter or very early spring with a string trimmer.

CHAPTER 2:
PLANTING A HEALTHY LAWN

A healthy lawn that looks great with a minimum of care isn't an impossible dream. Whether you're starting a new lawn from scratch or replacing an existing one, getting it off to a good start is an all-important first step. By preparing the soil well and selecting an appropriate turfgrass, you're well on your way to an attractive, durable lawn. Add moderate amounts of thoughtful, timely care and you've got it made — without devoting your life or your pocketbook to lawn care.

CHOOSING THE BEST GRASS

The best way to reduce the maintenance requirements of your lawn is to grow a species of grass suited to your climate and to your tolerance for maintenance. There are species and cultivars that resist drought, insects, and diseases; ones that stand up to heavy foot traffic; and even types that need less frequent mowing.

To plant a lawn that is vigorous and easy to keep healthy, start by choosing the right type of grass for your area and preparing the soil properly. You can select and plant grasses that resist insects and diseases, tolerate heavy foot traffic, and grow well in adverse conditions such as shade or drought.

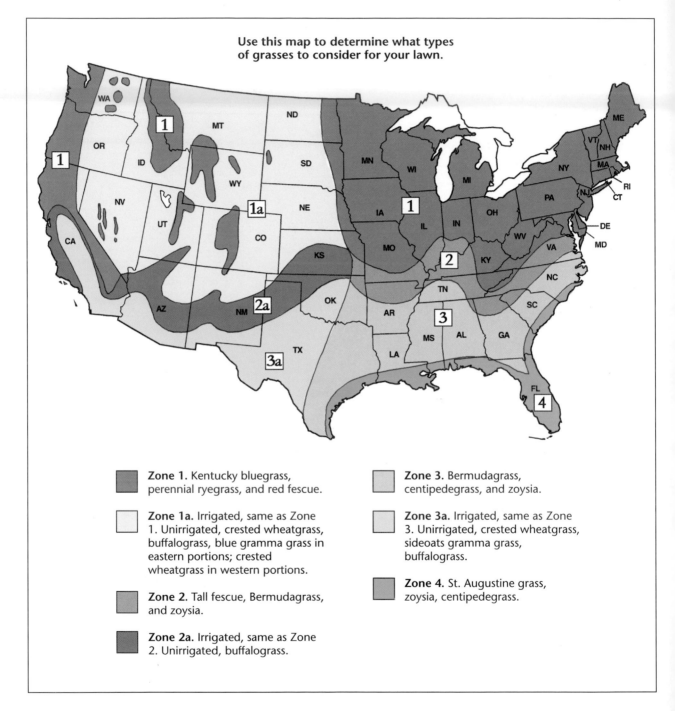

Use this map to determine what types of grasses to consider for your lawn.

Zone 1. Kentucky bluegrass, perennial ryegrass, and red fescue.

Zone 1a. Irrigated, same as Zone 1. Unirrigated, crested wheatgrass, buffalograss, blue gramma grass in eastern portions; crested wheatgrass in western portions.

Zone 2. Tall fescue, Bermudagrass, and zoysia.

Zone 2a. Irrigated, same as Zone 2. Unirrigated, buffalograss.

Zone 3. Bermudagrass, centipedegrass, and zoysia.

Zone 3a. Irrigated, same as Zone 3. Unirrigated, crested wheatgrass, sideoats gramma grass, buffalograss.

Zone 4. St. Augustine grass, zoysia, centipedegrass.

The range of choices can be overwhelming, and plant breeders are developing new lawn grasses every year. New lawn grasses are generally trademarked and cost more than generic types, but they are well worth the extra expense because they feature characteristics such as improved insect or disease resistance, more vigorous growth habits, or slower-growing, more compact habits that require less mowing. See "A Guide to Grasses" on page 29 for information on the most popular types of grasses, but before you install a new lawn, consult a local expert. Your extension service, a local landscape architect or contractor, or a knowledgeable person at a nursery or garden center can recommend the best and newest grasses for your area.

Lawn grasses are sold as seed, sod, sprigs, and plugs. The grasses that are most often used in American lawns are categorized in several ways: fine-bladed or coarse-bladed; sod-forming or bunching; warm-season or cool-season.

Fine-bladed grasses have blades that are less than $1/4$ inch wide; they're used

Buy the Best Seed

Before you buy a bag or box of lawn-grass seed, read the label carefully. It can tell you volumes about the quality of the seed. Since poor-quality seed takes just as much work to sow as good-quality seed, buy the best mix available. Look for blends of seed especially formulated for the type of site you have. Here are some tips from the Lawn Institute on what to look for:

■ Mixes that contain more than 15 percent annual ryegrass or annual bluegrass are generally poor quality.

■ Look for germination percentages above 85 percent. Check the date it was tested and only buy seed tested within the last year.

■ The best mixes have less than 1 percent "other crop" seed listed on the label. The Institute recommends that mixes contain *no* annual and rough bluegrass (*Poa annua* and *P. trivalis)* and no bentgrass.

■ Seed producers list percentages for nonnoxious and noxious weeds on the label. Buy mixes that contain *no* noxious weed seeds. Seeds of nonnoxious weeds are very difficult to remove entirely: a bag or box should contain between 0.3 and 0.5 percent by weight.

■ Inert matter, which includes broken seeds that will not germinate and fillers, should be well below 1 percent.

to create carpetlike lawns. Bentgrass, Kentucky bluegrass, and zoysia are the most common fine-textured grasses. Wider, coarse-bladed grasses (annual ryegrass, tall fescue, and St. Augustine grass) can look weedy, but they offer other redeeming qualities, such as durability and shade or drought tolerance.

Grasses also are classified by the way they grow. Sod-forming grasses spread by stolons (horizontal stems that creep above ground) or rhizomes (underground stems), filling in bare patches, forcing out weeds, and creating a thick lawn. Sod-forming grasses include bentgrass, Bermudagrass, and zoysia-grass. Bunchgrasses, by contrast, grow in clumps and spread only by expanding their basal growth. They are often fast growers that stand up well to traffic. Bunchgrasses, such as perennial ryegrass, tall fescue, and blue gramma grass, are sometimes mixed with sod-forming grasses.

The most basic division among lawn grasses describes their growth habits. Warm-season grasses, such as Bermudagrass and St. Augustine grass, grow rapidly in hot weather, but turn brown and go dormant when it's cool. Cool-season grasses (Kentucky bluegrass, bentgrass, perennial ryegrass, and the fescues) do the opposite. In dry areas in the West, many gardeners are turning to native grasses such as buffalograss and blue gramma grass. Both are warm-season grasses that will survive without irrigation. See the map on page 26 to determine which type of grass is most common in your region.

TIPS FOR SUCCESS

Special blends of lawn grasses are available for problem spots such as your children's backyard soccer or football field. Called sports turf, these mixes are designed to take extra wear and tear and still look attractive. They can include warm- or cool-season grasses and can be planted as part of a brand-new lawn or be seeded over an existing one. Consult your local cooperative extension service or a turfgrass specialist for the best selections for your area. Since soil compaction can become a problem on high-traffic sites, regular aeration is a good idea to ensure proper drainage and healthy roots.

A Guide to Warm-Season Grasses

- ### Bahiagrass

DESCRIPTION: Warm-season grass with generally coarse texture. Slow to germinate, but vigorous once established.

COMMENTS: This inexpensive grass doesn't make an ideal lawn, but it is the best warm-season grass for shade. A sharp mower is required to cut it cleanly. Sow 5 pounds seed per 1,000 square feet.

- ### Bermudagrass

DESCRIPTION: Warm-season grass with coarse to fine texture and vigorous growth habit. Turns brown after frost. Overseeding with fine fescues or perennial ryegrass will maintain green winter color.

COMMENTS: Bermudagrass is easily invaded by weeds in winter when it is dormant; overseeding helps prevent this. It is difficult to keep out of flower beds and borders. Sow 1–3 pounds seed per 1,000 square feet; some improved types are only available as sod, plugs, or sprigs.

- ### Blue gramma grass

DESCRIPTION: Warm-season, low-growing bunching grass with medium to fine texture.

COMMENTS: This drought-tolerant grass will grow well in alkaline soils. It turns brown in severe drought. Sow 1–1$\frac{1}{2}$ pounds seed per 1,000 square feet.

Buffalograss is a drought-resistant native grass that spreads by stolons. It makes an ideal low-maintenance lawn for the Great Plains.

■ Buffalograss

DESCRIPTION: Warm-season native grass with fine texture. It spreads by stolons, but grows slowly and is less invasive than Bermudagrass.

COMMENTS: Buffalograss tolerates heavy clay soil and drought. It goes dormant and turns brown in summer and again in fall. It is used as a low-maintenance alternative to Bermudagrass. Sow 5–7 pounds seed per 1,000 square feet.

■ Carpetgrass

DESCRIPTION: Warm-season grass with coarse texture that spreads vigorously by stolons.

COMMENTS: Will grow in poor, sandy soil, but does not tolerate drought or cold temperatures. It will tolerate heavy traffic. Disease- and insect-resistant types are available. Sow 3–4 pounds seed per 1,000 square feet.

■ Centipedegrass

DESCRIPTION: Warm-season grass with coarse to medium texture. Spreads to form a dense sod, but does not grow as rapidly as other warm-season grasses.

COMMENTS: Resists insects and diseases and requires less mowing and fertilizing than other warm-season grasses. Sow $\frac{1}{4}$–1 pound per 1,000 square feet; some improved types are only available as sod, plugs, or sprigs.

▪ St. Augustine grass

DESCRIPTION: Warm-season, coarse-textured grass. Spreads to form a dense sod, but prone to thatch development.

COMMENTS: Requires fertile soil and plenty of water. New insect-resistant types are available. It is prone to thatch buildup. Shade-tolerant. Plant sod or sprigs; does not set seed.

Zoysia is a warm-season grass that spreads by stolons and rhizomes to form dense, weed-resistant sod.

▪ Zoysiagrass

DESCRIPTION: Warm-season grass with coarse to fine texture. Spreads by stolons and rhizomes. Turns brown after frost and greens up slowly in spring.

COMMENTS: Zoysia grows very slowly, but is prone to developing thatch. Tolerates traffic and resists weeds. Slow-growing. Somewhat drought-tolerant, but requires watering in dry areas. Plant sod or sprigs only.

A GUIDE TO COOL-SEASON GRASSES

▪ Fine Fescues

DESCRIPTION: Cool-season grasses with fine texture. Two types, chewings fescue and red fescue, are available.

COMMENTS: Tolerate shade and drought. Disease- and insect-resistant selections are available. Sow 3–4 pounds seed per 1,000 square feet.

Kentucky bluegrass is probably the most popular lawn grass in North America. It tolerates heat, cold, and drought and forms dense, deep green sod.

▪ Kentucky bluegrass

DESCRIPTION: Cool-season grass with fine to medium texture. Its spreading rhizomes form dense sod. Greens up well in spring.

COMMENTS: Many improved cultivars with multiple disease resistance are available. Cultivars also have been selected for regional adaptability; plant the best ones for your area. Most are not shade-tolerant. Sow 1–2 pounds seed per 1,000 square feet.

- **Perennial ryegrass**

DESCRIPTION: Cool-season grass with medium to fine texture. Fast-growing and vigorous.

COMMENTS: Tolerates heat, cold, heavy traffic, and will grow in considerable shade. Improved types with resistance to many insects and diseases are available. Sow 4–6 pounds seed per 1,000 square feet.

- **Tall Fescuc**

DESCRIPTION: Cool-season bunching grass with coarse to medium texture. Does not form thatch.

COMMENTS: Tolerates shade, heat, heavy traffic, and a wide range of soils. Disease- and insect-resistant selections are available. Sow 5–8 pounds seed per 1,000 square feet.

PREPARING THE SOIL

The most carefully chosen and tended grass will not grow well unless the soil beneath it is reasonably healthy. Regrading, loosening compacted soil, adding organic matter, and improving drainage are all much more difficult once the lawn is in place, so take time for these steps before you sow seed, lay sod, or plant sprigs or plugs.

Grading. Before you think about adding amendments or loosening up the soil, check the grade. Ideally, the soil surface should drop away from your house in all directions, about 1 foot for every 100 feet of distance. Water may stand on flatter grades or run off steeper ones.

Few gardeners are blessed with an ideal site. Fortunately, small grade problems, such as bumps, potholes, or low spots, can often be corrected with a shovel, rake, wheelbarrow, and some elbow grease. Major changes require heavy equip-

Scrimping on soil preparation before planting a new lawn will only lead to problems down the road. Check the grade of your site, then have the soil tested. Loosen the soil, incorporate recommended amendments, rake the site smooth, and you are ready to plant.

ment, which can be expensive and disruptive. If you're building a new house or overhauling an existing landscape, talk with the builder or a landscape contractor about making major changes to improve conditions. Soil around new houses usually has been compacted by heavy construction equipment. Make sure that the builder remedies this by loosening the soil as deeply as possible, with tractor-drawn equipment if necessary: simply spreading a few inches of topsoil over a rock-hard surface is a sure-fire recipe for a problem-prone lawn.

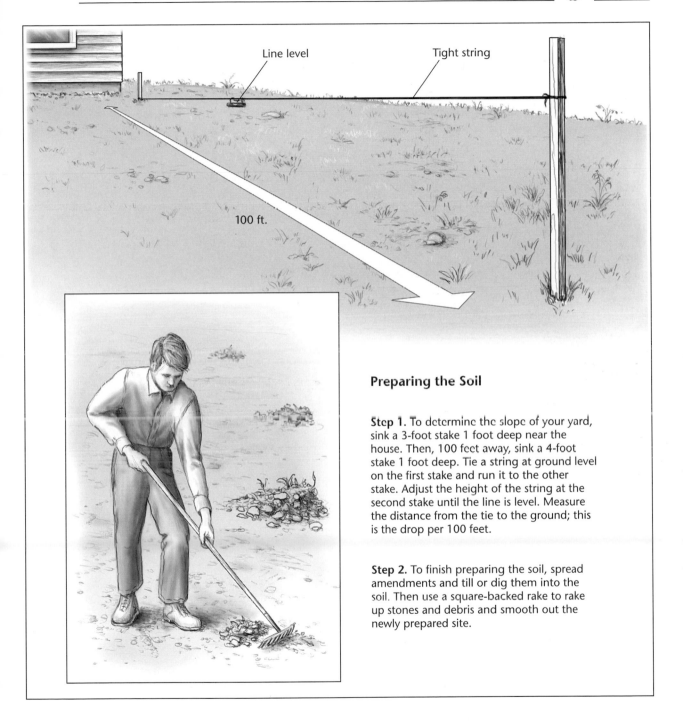

Line level

Tight string

100 ft.

Preparing the Soil

Step 1. To determine the slope of your yard, sink a 3-foot stake 1 foot deep near the house. Then, 100 feet away, sink a 4-foot stake 1 foot deep. Tie a string at ground level on the first stake and run it to the other stake. Adjust the height of the string at the second stake until the line is level. Measure the distance from the tie to the ground; this is the drop per 100 feet.

Step 2. To finish preparing the soil, spread amendments and till or dig them into the soil. Then use a square-backed rake to rake up stones and debris and smooth out the newly prepared site.

If regrading isn't practical, consider other solutions. Terraces can create flat or gently sloping areas on a steep site. If the property is relatively flat but too damp, or if there are swales or depressions where water collects, consider installing drain lines. See chapter 1, "Planning a Low-Maintenance Lawn," for more ideas on what to do with problem sites.

Soil improvement. There is nothing mysterious about a lawn's fertility needs. Like other plants, grasses need soil rich in nitrogen, phosphorus, and potassium. Take the time to test your soil, sending the samples to your state's extension service lab or to a reputable private lab. Be sure to specify that the test is for a lawn and ask for organic recommendations.

Most grasses prefer a neutral pH, in the range of 6.5 to 7.5. Your soil test should indicate how much (if any) limestone or sulfur you need to add to raise or lower the pH of your soil. Your results will also indicate nutrient deficiencies and recommended amendments.

Simple Soil Tests

An easy way to assess your soil's texture (its sand, silt, and clay content) is to take a handful of moist earth and feel how it responds when you rub and squeeze it. If it feels gritty, it is high in sand. If it feels sticky, it's high in clay. Sandy soils tend to drain quickly, and they benefit from added organic matter (such as compost), which helps retain water and nutrients for healthy plant growth. Clay soils, on the other hand, tend to hold too much water, promoting root rots and other disease problems. Adding organic matter here, too, will help, by loosening the soil and improving drainage.

To test the soil's overall drainage, dig one or more test holes about 2 feet deep. Fill the hole(s) with water and check to see if any water remains in the bottom of the hole after 24 hours. If all the water is gone, the drainage is fine. If just a little water remains, the drainage will be adequate for some plants but not for all. If most of the water remains, drainage is so poor that you'll either need to install an underground drain system or select plants that naturally thrive in wet soil.

Before adding any amendments, though, take a close look at your soil's structure. Knowing whether you are working with sand, clay, loam, or something in between will aid you in choosing grass types and in setting your irrigation schedule. (See "Simple Soil Tests" on page 36 for easy ways to test soil texture and drainage.) If your soil contains a large amount of clay or sand, plan to dig or till at least a 2-inch layer of organic matter (compost, peat moss, or dried manure, for instance) before spreading other amendments. Or spread a 3-inch layer of rich topsoil and incorporate it into your soil by digging or tilling.

Spread the amendments recommended by your soil test (lime or sulfur to adjust the pH and amendments to correct nutrient deficiencies or improve overall fertility) over the soil and till to a depth of 6 inches. Or make one or two passes with a tractor-mounted disk. If your test was in the normal range, till or dig the soil to loosen it, then broadcast a starter fertilizer over the area; use a prepackaged organic fertilizer such as processed manure or 25 pounds each of blood meal, bone meal, and greensand per 1,000 square feet. After incorporating amendments, rake the surface smooth.

At this point, the soil will be rather soft and in need of settling. To speed the process, rent a roller (basically a big barrel with handles attached). Fill the barrel one-third to one-half full of water and roll it over the soil to smooth and firm it. Don't wait too long to plant after rolling; a heavy downpour can wash away bare soil in the wink of an eye.

Eliminating weeds. The more weeds you can eradicate before installing a lawn, the fewer you'll have to deal with later. Through a process called solarization you can kill weed seeds and seedlings when you prepare your soil. Stretch a sheet — or several — of clear plastic tightly over tilled and thoroughly watered soil. Leave the plastic in place for about four weeks. Solarization will kill weeds and weed seeds in the top layer of soil. Since it requires hot, sunny weather to be effective you will have to time your sowing schedule accordingly.

Another way to eliminate weeds is by successive tillings. Your first tilling will destroy established weeds while bringing new weed seeds to the surface to germinate. Wait at least two weeks until a solid crop of new weeds sprouts, then do them in with another tilling. Two or three tillings will eliminate many of the resident weeds.

The main advantage of using sod is that it creates an instant lawn. Sod is expensive and takes time and energy to lay properly. Once it is in place, though, all you need to do is keep the sod moist until the roots knit into the soil and you have a finished lawn.

PLANTING OPTIONS

You can start a new lawn from seed, sod, sprigs, or plugs. Seeding is the cheapest, easiest, and most common method, and it offers the greatest choice of turfgrass types. If you need a lawn in a hurry, sod is best, but it is much more expensive and takes more work. Sprigs and plugs (individual grass plants or parts of plants) are less expensive than sod, because you do not plant them in a solid blanket. But they demand patience. It may take several years for plugs to fill in

Seeding a new lawn is inexpensive and fairly easy once the soil is prepared. Cover the seed with weed-free straw and keep the soil moist, even if it means watering lightly several times a day, until the seedlings are 2 inches tall. Leave the straw to rot on the lawn; it will disappear quickly.

and cover an area. In the meantime, you have to keep the remaining bare soil free of weeds.

Whether you're starting from seed, sod, sprigs, or plugs, you will have to know the total square footage of the area in order to determine how much to buy. Measure the site and calculate the total square footage (length × width = square feet). See "A Guide to Grasses" on page 29 for recommended seed-sowing rates. The amount of sod you need will depend on the size of the pieces you buy, and the number of sprigs or plugs on the recommended spacing.

Seeding a Lawn

The best time to sow a lawn is when the young grass plants will have an advantage over weeds. In the North, the best time is autumn, at least six weeks before the first frost. The cool-season grasses are ready to take off once the heat breaks, but most annual weeds are not programmed to germinate in the fall. Northerners can also sow in early spring, as soon as the ground can be worked, which will give the grass plenty of time to establish itself before the summer heat sets in. In the South, sow warm-season grasses in late spring or early summer and cool-season grasses in late summer or early fall.

Sowing in Shade

It is possible to grow a healthy lawn in moderate shade if you do it correctly right from the start. Before you plant, make sure that the soil is fertile and well drained, and remove all perennial weed roots from the top 6 inches of the soil. Then plant a suitable type of grass. Check at your nursery to find out what shade-tolerant grasses do best in your area. In general, fescues handle the shade well; Kentucky bluegrass does not. You will find blends of grass seed formulated for shade.

Use them; don't simply fill the site with a leftover mix you have on hand.

Once the grass is up, care for it differently than if it were growing in full sun. Since low light levels cut down on how much food the plants can manufacture, increase the leaf surface by mowing 1 inch higher than the recommended height for full sun. Provide a little extra fertilizer and water. If necessary, prune nearby trees and shrubs to increase air circulation.

Sowing Grass Seed

Whether you spread grass seed by hand or with a broadcast seeder, make sure you spread it as evenly as possible. The best way is to divide the seed into two batches and make two passes over the lawn at right angles to each other.

When you've decided what type of grass to plant, take a close look at the labels of the various brands. Grass seed is generally sold as a blend that contains a mix of different cultivars, each contributing one or more important qualities. Find out what types of seed are in the mix and what characteristics they feature. Look for named cultivars of seed whenever possible — 'Estate' or 'Merit' Kentucky bluegrass, for example, rather than just a generic Kentucky bluegrass. The label should list the species and cultivars included, the percentage of each, and whether they are fine- or coarse-textured. See "Buy the Best Seed" on page 27 for tips that will guide you to the best-quality mixes. If you have a mix of sunny and shady spots to sow, buy a mix especially formulated for each area.

The easiest and most accurate way to sow grass seed is with a broadcast or drop spreader, but you can also do a perfectly acceptable job by hand. When you're ready to sow, divide the seed into two equal portions. Put half in the spreader or, if you're sowing by hand, in a bucket. Make one pass over the area with the first batch of seed. Then with the rest of the seed, make a second pass at right angles to the first. This will give you good coverage.

After sowing all the seed, rake a thin layer of soil over it. Firm down the seedbed with a lawn roller or tamp it with the back of a rake. To keep the soil moist, which is critical for germination, cover it thinly with weed-free straw. (Hay contains weed seed; peat moss and sawdust crust over into an impenetrable layer.)

Don't allow the soil surface to dry out until the grass is 2 inches tall, even if you must water it lightly several times a day. But be careful not to saturate the soil. When the grass emerges, stay off it, and do not mow until it is 2 to 3 inches high. (Leave the straw to rot.) Then treat it as you would an established lawn.

Laying Sod

The best time for laying sod is fall or early spring in the North, spring in the South. Never plant during hot, dry weather — you can't afford to let the sod dry out before its roots have knitted into the soil. Always prepare the soil *before* you have the sod delivered so you can plant it right away.

It's just as important to start with good sod as with good seed. Buy sod guaranteed to be free of insects, diseases, and weeds. Ask what species of grass are in the sod and look for sod grown from improved cultivars that perform well in your area. Inspect the sod carefully, if possible, before it is delivered. Pieces should be green, moist, and firm, with a thick set of roots. Reject any sod that is sparse, brown, yellow, or flimsy. Sod that is too thick — more than 1 inch — doesn't establish well either. Sod that is 3/4 inch thick is ideal.

> **TIPS FOR SUCCESS**
>
> If you are comparing prices, ask what size pieces you are buying: Sod is cut in widths ranging from 14 to 24 inches and pieces can be from 24 to 72 inches long. Rolled sod tends to be easier to carry than folded sod.

Prepare the soil for sod exactly as you would for seed, including rolling it. The night before laying the sod, water the area thoroughly (ideally to a depth of 8 inches). Water uniformly and gently to prevent puddles and mud from forming.

Lay sod as quickly as possible; if it sits in a pile and heats up, the roots may

Laying Sod

Step 1. When laying sod, line up the pieces as closely and neatly as possible, but stagger the ends of the pieces from row to row as if you were building a brick wall. Kneel on a piece of plywood instead of on the freshly laid sod.

Step 2. Smooth soil into the joints between the pieces of sod with a trowel. Then use a lawn roller to ensure firm contact between the grass roots and the soil. Keep the soil moist by watering during the warmest part of the day until the roots have grown into the soil.

be permanently damaged. If you can't finish on the day of delivery, store the remainder in a cool, shaded place and lay it first thing the next day.

Laying sod is a bit like building a brick wall, and it requires some precision. Lay the first course in a straight line — against the edge of a walk or a driveway, or a string stretched between two stakes. Butt the ends and edges of the strips tightly together without overlap. Stagger the joints of adjacent courses. If you need to work on top of laid sod, place a piece of plywood on it to distribute your weight and prevent damage.

Once the sod is in place, spread a thin layer of topsoil over the sod, working the soil into the cracks with a broom or the back of a wooden rake. Then go over it once or twice with a light lawn roller. Keep the sod moist by watering during the warmest part of each day until the roots have knitted into the soil; you can pull up a corner to check.

If you lay sod on a slope, orient the long edges of the sod across rather than up and down the slope. If pieces slip, peg them in place with wooden stakes or large staples made from coat hangers. (Pull the pegs or staples out before you use the roller.)

Planting Plugs and Sprigs

Some grasses, such as zoysias, St. Augustine, and improved selections of Bermuda-grass, aren't readily available from seed. They can be planted as sod, but are also commonly planted as plugs or sprigs. Plugs are 2- to 3-inch cubes of turf that are planted in a checkerboard pattern. You can buy plugs in trays or make them

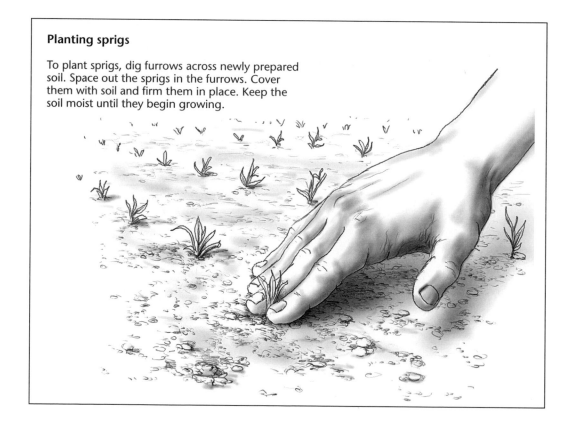

Planting sprigs

To plant sprigs, dig furrows across newly prepared soil. Space out the sprigs in the furrows. Cover them with soil and firm them in place. Keep the soil moist until they begin growing.

yourself by cutting apart sod. Sprigs are small sections of stems with roots attached. You can buy them by the bushel or make your own by shredding pieces of sod. Because bare patches of soil are left between plugs and sprigs, which the grass will eventually fill in, plugging and sprigging require less sod and cost less than sodding. They do, however, require more work because weeds growing between the grass plants must be controlled until the grass fills in.

Before planting either plugs or sprigs, prepare the soil as for seeding. To plant plugs, use a plugging tool, which is a sort of miniature posthole digger that makes it easy to dig a hole for each plug. (You may be able to rent one.) The plugs may take anywhere from a few weeks to a year or two to fill in completely. Plugs of most warm-season grasses are spaced about 18 inches apart; zoysia takes longer to spread and should be spaced about 12 inches apart. Plant sprigs in regularly spaced, 3- to 4-inch-deep furrows. As with plugs, spacing depends on the type of grass you are planting. Bermudagrass, centipedegrass, and St. Augustine grass usually are spaced 1 foot apart; zoysia sprigs are spaced 6 inches apart. Sprigs can also be planted end-to-end in rows. Cover the sprigs with 1/4 inch of topsoil.

After planting, roll the lawn and water thoroughly. Keep the soil evenly moist until they begin growing. Use a hoe to keep weeds controlled until the plugs or sprigs have filled in.

Chapter 3:
Caring for Your Lawn

Maintaining a lawn is like caring for a house or an automobile — a little regular attention can prevent major headaches later on. By promptly and properly mowing, watering, fertilizing — as well as attending to weeds, insects, or diseases — you can keep your lawn healthy without spending a great deal of time or money. See Chapter 5 for information on insect, disease, and weed control. For tips on reducing the time it takes to care for your lawn, see "Reducing Maintenance" on page 64.

Mowing

Most people cut their grass purely for aesthetic reasons. But there's much more at stake than just keeping your lawn tidy and attractive. How and when you cut your grass can make the difference between a healthy lawn and an ailing one.

A grass plant, of course, grows just like other plants. The larger its above-

Routine maintenance will keep your lawn vigorous and healthy for years to come. To water efficiently and effectively, water early in the morning and soak the soil deeply to encourage grass roots to grow deep into the soil.

ground parts, the more food it produces and the longer its roots grow. Mowing shocks grass, no matter how high or low the cut. But when grass blades are cut too short, food production drops and roots may stop growing altogether. The weakened plants are more susceptible to disease and the stress of heat or drought.

When in doubt, follow these two mowing rules and you won't go far wrong. First, never remove more than one-third of the top growth at any one time. For example, trim only 1 inch off 3-inch-tall grass; any more will weaken the grass. Second, mow high and mow often. Studies have shown that high and frequent mowing imparts the greatest vigor, creating a healthier lawn with fewer weeds.

How high to mow. Ideal mowing height varies by species and cultivar. Some grasses are naturally low-growing and do best when kept short. Let them grow long, and you'll get thatch buildup, seed-head formation, and a poor appearance. Others do better when cut high. Bermudagrass, carpetgrass, centipedegrass, blue

Keep Those Clippings

Until recently, most homeowners bagged and discarded grass clippings as a matter of course. But clippings actually provide fertilizer for your lawn. They contain a significant amount of nutrients, especially nitrogen, which return to the lawn when the clippings decompose. (By some estimates, you can reduce your lawn's fertilizer requirements by 25 percent if you leave clippings where they fall.) Keep in mind, too, that clippings from properly managed lawns do not contribute to thatch, which consists primarily of the tougher parts of the grass plants such as the stems, stolons, and rhizomes.

To prevent unsightly mats of fresh clippings from accumulating and smothering grass beneath them, cut the lawn when the grass is dry, and cut it before it grows more than 1 inch taller than its recommended mowing height. Mulching mowers are designed to chop up the clippings to speed their decomposition, but clippings from conventional mowers disappear quickly as well if the grass isn't too long. If the length of your grass gets out of hand after a vacation or rainy spell, bag your clippings and use them to mulch your vegetable garden. Or add them to the compost pile. Otherwise, you'll be throwing away free fertilizer.

gramma grass, and zoysia should be cut to between $\frac{1}{2}$ and 2 inches. Cut buffalograss, fine fescues, and perennial ryegrass to between 2 and $2\frac{1}{2}$ inches. Bahiagrass, Kentucky bluegrass, and St. Augustine grass should be cut to between 2 and 3 inches tall. Tall fescue can be cut to anywhere between 2 and 4 inches.

Because vigorously growing grass can bounce back from stress, you can mow lower than the ideal in the spring and fall in the North, when cool-season grasses are most active, and during the summer in the South, when warm-season grasses are most vigorous. During other seasons, when the grass naturally slows down, or when times are tough, as during heat and drought, mow higher.

Selecting a mower. Most homeowners use rotary mowers to cut their lawn. These cut with a blade that sweeps through the grass. The new mulching-type mowers

Mowing up Leaves

A bagging lawn mower comes in handy for "mowing" leaves off the lawn in fall. The chopped leaves make excellent winter mulch for perennial gardens.

are specially designed to chop up grass clippings into fine particles so they will decompose quickly. Rotary mowers are easy to maintain, can be adjusted to various mowing heights, and are fairly easy to use. Be sure to keep the blade sharp: A dull blade tears off the tops of the grass, causing it more stress and resulting in a grayish lawn. Most mowers should be sharpened monthly during the growing season; some mulching mowers have blades that simply need replacing once a year. If you have hilly terrain to mow, self-propelled mowers are especially helpful. Although clippings should most often be left on the lawn, a bagging mower is handy if the grass has gotten too tall.

Reel mowers cut grass with a scissoring action that cuts grass more cleanly than rotary mowers and damages the grass less. They are quiet and pleasurable to use, something that is appealing in these days of power garden equipment. While old reel mowers may be cranky and hard to keep adjusted, new models are well engineered and worth considering — especially if you have a small lawn. On the downside, reel mowers have trouble cutting grass longer than 2 inches or grasses that send up tall seed heads, such as bahiagrass and St. Augustine grass. They also cannot cut tough grasses, such as ryegrass, cleanly. Tough, stalky weeds, such as plantain, are also troublesome.

WATERING

When it comes to watering, many people are guilty of killing their lawns with kindness. The worst thing you can do to your lawn is to sprinkle it lightly and frequently. Grass that is watered in this manner won't put down deep roots, and if the water supply is cut off, the shallow roots dry out quickly and the grass wilts and may die.

Think of watering as refilling the reservoir in the soil rather than sprinkling the grass. Grass needs as much as 1 to 2 inches of water per week to grow, but in many parts of the country nature provides much of that. The trick is to water deeply when you water at all, and to water only when the grass absolutely needs it — when the water reservoir in the soil is just about dry. A good rule of thumb is to provide an inch of water in a single soaking per week. With increased concern about water conservation, many gardeners are deciding to water only when the grass absolutely needs it. The lawn will tell you when it's time: blades will

Sprinkler Options

In-ground irrigation systems are expensive to install, but may be practical in regions where lawn grasses need regular watering. Pop-up spray heads are forced up by water pressure when the water is turned on and drop back down when it is off. Use fixed-riser spray heads for areas planted with ground covers. If used in a lawn, they will make mowing difficult.

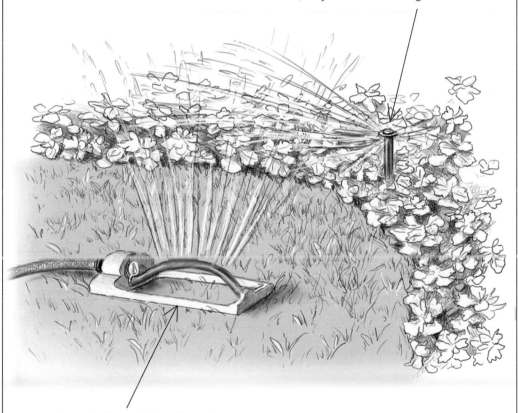

An oscillating sprinkler allows for slow penetration of water into the soil and covers a large square or rectangular area. It throws water high into the air, however, where it can be lost through evaporation or carried away by wind.

More Sprinkler Options

Traveling sprinklers move along the hose, watering as they go. They provide excellent coverage and save you the trouble of moving the sprinkler around the lawn.

Impulse sprinklers cover circular areas with a reliable and even coverage rate. Since they force water out at fairly high pressure, they will cover a large area.

begin to wilt, their color will become dull, and the turf won't spring back when you walk on it.

Watering without waste. A great deal of water is wasted on lawns. Sprinklers are too often whirling during the hottest part of the day, when much water is lost to evaporation, or they're left on after the soil is saturated, and water runs off into the storm sewers. When you irrigate a lawn, you should always water slowly so that the water has time to seep into the soil without running off the surface. A sprinkler with a low flow rate (less than $1/4$ inch per hour) will minimize runoff. To determine how

> **TIPS FOR SUCCESS**
>
> Keep in mind that the type of soil you have will affect the amount of water your lawn will need. Clay soils can store more water than loamy soils, and loamy soils can store more water than sandy ones. The more water the soil can store, the less often it will need watering.

long a sprinkler takes to deliver an inch of water, spread some empty 1-inch-deep tuna cans under the sprinkler and see how long it takes them to fill. Early morning watering minimizes evaporation (because the air is cool) and gives the blades time to dry off during the day, reducing the chance of fungal infections.

There are alternatives to watering. In the North, most grasses will survive a summer without watering by going dormant. They may stop growing, and even turn brown, but once the weather cools and the rain returns in the fall, they will come back to life. In the South, Bermudagrass is relatively drought-tolerant. buffalograss and blue gramma grass are even more so.

For those inevitable times, then, when you forget to water and the lawn turns brown, chances are good that the grass is not dead, but has gone dormant and will bounce back once it is watered.

FERTILIZING

After years of recommending that homeowners pour on fertilizer spring, summer, and fall, experts are now concluding that we feed our lawns too much. True, grass that doesn't get enough fertilizer grows slowly and sparsely; it loses the battle against certain weeds and is more vulnerable to damage from insects, disease, and drought. But overfertilized grass has problems as well, some of them the same

Using Organic Fertilizers

Use the results of your soil test to figure out how much fertilizer you need to spread. This is relatively simple and requires only basic arithmetic. The easiest way to explain the calculations is by example: Let's say the soil-test report recommends 2 pounds of actual nitrogen per 1,000 square feet. You are fertilizing 100 square feet with a 5-10-10 fertilizer (the numbers indicate the percentages of nitrogen, phosphate, and potassium). How much should you apply?

Start by asking how much 5 percent fertilizer it takes to supply 2 pounds of nitrogen. Set up a simple equation, using x as the unknown amount of fertilizer:

$$.05x = 2 \text{ lb.}$$
$$x = 2 \div .05$$
$$x = 40 \text{ lb.}$$

It will take 40 pounds of a 5-10-10 fertilizer per 1,000 square feet to supply 2 pounds of nitrogen. Since you are fertilizing one-tenth as much area, you need to spread only 4 pounds of a 5-10-10 fertilizer to meet the lab's nitrogen recommendation. Calculations for the other elements are, of course, done in the same manner.

You can buy a pre-blended organic fertilizer or use the chart on the facing page to determine which organic fertilizers to mix to provide the nutrient levels your lawn needs.

as those caused by too little fertilizer — reduced root growth and drought resistance, increased susceptibility to pests and diseases, and thatch formation.

Grass grows best when it receives a slow, steady supply of fertilizer. How much and when depends on the type of grass and the climate. In the North, most turfgrasses can get by with one or two applications of a slow-acting fertilizer annually. In the South, grass grows best with two or three small doses during the growing season.

Fertilizer	Nitrogen	Phosphorus	Potassium	Application rate (per 100 sq. ft.)
Activated sewage sludge (Milorganite)	4–6%	2–4%	trace	4–6 lb.
Alfalfa pellets	2.7%	0.5%	2.8%	5 lb.
Blood meal	9–14%	1.6%	0.84%	2 lb.
Bone meal	2%	25–30%	0%	4 lb.
Cottonseed meal	6–7%	2–3%	1–2%	5 lb.
Fish emulsion	12%	0%	1%	25 gal. (1 tbsp./gal.)
Fish meal	4–9%	7%	trace	2–4 lb.
Manure, dried				
Cow	2%	1.8%	2.2%	6–8 lb.
Horse	0.7%	0.3%	0.6%	6–8 lb.
Poultry	6%	4%	3%	2 lb.
Seaweed extract (kelp)	2%	1%	4–13%	2–3 lb.
Soybean meal	6%	1%	2%	4–5 lb.
Wood ash	0%	trace	5–10%	5 lb.

In the North, the best time to fertilize is September or October. This will help the plant roots create and store enough food to get the plant off to a good start in the spring. If you don't have to feed grass in the spring, you'll deny hungry young weeds free food. Alternatively, you can give northern grass a half-dose in the spring (May or June) and another in the fall.

Warm-season grasses, on the other hand, are natural summer feeders. Their requirements vary more than do those of northern grasses. Some types can do

Raking Options

Raking up fallen leaves is a time-honored fall chore that is important to your lawn's health. Wet leaves will pack down on a lawn over winter and smother it, leaving you with problems to repair in spring. There are a variety of ways to speed up the raking process, though. You can mow leaves off the lawn with a bagging lawn mower, although you will have to pause frequently to empty the bag. Or blow them off with a side-discharge mower. Just make a series of passes with the discharge chute always facing the same direction and you'll gradually move the leaves off the lawn. An old king-size bed sheet makes a handy tool if you still favor conventional raking. Rake the leaves onto it, gather up the four corners, and you can haul off several bushels at a time.

quite well with two feedings, one in early summer, perhaps June, and one in late summer, around August. Others need feeding every month. But again, the more frequent the feedings, the smaller the dose of fertilizer required.

Different types of grass need different amounts of fertilizer. Bentgrass, a heavy feeder, requires 2 to 4 pounds of actual nitrogen for each 1,000 square feet per year. (It is used for golf greens but isn't a practical lawn grass.) Others, such as buffalograss and fine fescue, require only half as much, while Bermudagrass and Kentucky bluegrass fall between the two extremes.

When you fertilize your lawn, it's best to follow the old organic gardening principle of feeding the soil instead of the plant. Manures, composts, and other plant and animal residues all improve the physical structure of the soil and add organic matter that feed earthworms and soil microorganisms, which in turn feed the grass. There are new blended organic fertilizers on the market every year, and they are as easy to apply as chemical fertilizers — and much better for your soil. Get advice on amounts from your nursery or extension agent, or follow the recommendations on the fertilizer bag. Or you can use the chart on page 55 and the results of your soil test to mix your own fertilizer.

To distribute fertilizer across the lawn, you'll need a spreader. The two types commonly used are the drop spreader and the rotary spreader. A drop spreader drops a trail of fertilizer behind it as wide as its hopper. A rotary spreader uses a propellerlike device to sling fertilizer out. It takes a lot longer to cover the lawn using a drop spreader. But it's much more precise than a rotary spreader, which often scatters fertilizer on walks, driveways, ground covers, and flowers.

EDGING AND TRIMMING

Edging and trimming the lawn probably aren't high on many homeowners' lists of favorite activities, but they are all-important steps in creating a neat-looking lawn. Long-handled grass shears eliminate the need to crawl along the edges of your lawn on hands and knees, trimming grass as you go. String trimmers are noisier, but they make neatening up the edges of your yard fast and easy.

Installing edging strips to keep grass from spreading into flower gardens or ground covers not only reduces weeding and edging chores, but can also reduce

Use Trimmers Wisely

String trimmers make it easy to trim grass and weeds along buildings, raised beds, and other obstacles. Avoid using them to trim around trees and shrubs, because they can damage the bark. Instead, mulch around trees and shrubs and keep lawn grass away from the bases of easily damaged plants.

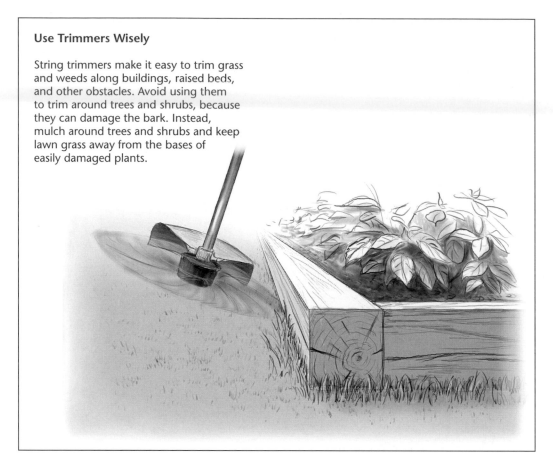

the time it takes to trim the lawn. Keep a mulched strip just inside the edging strip so you can run one wheel of your mower in the bed and trim along the edge of the grass all at one time — no extra time spent hand trimming. Plastic edging strips work fine, but aluminum ones are also available. Brick edging strips are ornamental but more expensive and time-consuming to install.

Eliminate Edging with Edging Strips

Edging strips installed flush with the soil around flower beds make it easy to mow and trim in one step: keep one wheel of the mower on the edging strip.

Edging Tools

The right tool can make all the difference when it comes to edging. An edging tool has a sharp cutting edge that slices away sod easily. A sharp spade is also effective. Both allow you to cut a neat, straight edge.

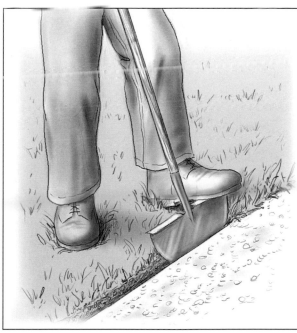

CHAPTER 4:
RENOVATING A LAWN

From time to time, even the healthiest lawn will show symptoms of wear, such as thin spots or bare patches. Cold, heat, drought, insects, and diseases all take their toll. A shabby lawn may be choked with thatch or suffering from compacted soil caused by hordes of football playing children. Or, you may have purchased a home with a lawn that has simply been neglected.

Fortunately, you don't necessarily have to start all over to have a healthy, lush lawn again. There are a variety of ways to renovate a lawn without ripping it out and starting over completely. For damaged patches of lawn, reseeding or resodding may be the answer. Aerating and top-dressing are two techniques that help improve the health and vitality of a tired-looking lawn. Or if your old lawn is in fair shape, with less than 25 percent weeds, the easiest way to renovate it is simply to overseed. But for lawns that have more weeds than grass, getting rid of all the old sod, thatch, and weeds and starting over is the best strategy.

If your lawn is less than perfect, you don't necessarily need to tear it out and start over to grow attractive turf like this. Eliminating thatch, aerating, and top-dressing will help restore ragged-looking turf. Overseeding with new, improved grasses that feature disease or pest resistance is another option.

WHAT'S THE PROBLEM?

Before you reseed, repair, or replace, you should first determine what is causing the problem. Spend some time examining the trouble spot and doing some detective work to decide why the problem has occurred. Determine if pests or diseases caused the problem, or if other factors are at work. Here are some common cultural problems to look for.

Thatch. The first sign of trouble to look for is thatch. Thatch is an impenetrable mat, mainly made up of roots, stolons, and rhizomes of grass plants that fail to decompose normally. Thick thatch prevents water from reaching the grass roots, and it harbors insects and diseases. By blocking light penetration, it also weakens the grass and prevents turf from spreading as it should. To check your grass for thatch, take a walk on your lawn with a ruler in your hand. First, get a feel for the lawn under your feet. If it is springy rather than firm, or if your feet sink deeply into the turf, you should suspect thatch. Look down at the lawn. You should be able to see soil between the grass plants. If, instead, you see a layer of tan, strawlike organic matter, your lawn has thatch. Use the ruler to measure the depth of the strawlike layer. If it is less than $1/4$ inch, it is not thick enough to cause any problems. If it is between $1/4$ and $1/2$ inch, it has the potential to become a problem. If it is more than $1/2$ inch thick, it is time to do something about it. See "Dealing with Thatch" on page 69.

Wet soil or poor drainage. A damaged patch of grass may be caused by poor soil drainage or something as simple as a leaking hose. If you suspect drainage and compaction problems, dig a hole about a foot deep and fill it with water. The water should begin to drain out immediately, and it should be completely gone by the next day. If it is not, aerating the soil (see page 71) and adding organic matter will help improve drainage. Or consider replacing lawn grasses with moisture-loving ground covers. Installing drain tiles under the lawn will improve drainage if you can't replace the lawn with ground covers or other plantings.

Heavy traffic. Trouble spots can be the result of heavy foot traffic. If so, consider sowing a tougher grass, such as tall fescue or a "sports turf" blend. Or eliminate turf in the area altogether and replace it with a flagstone or brick walk. Weak

It's difficult or impossible to grow a lawn on sites where cars drive or park even occasionally, but most homeowners don't want to pave such areas. Pre-cast paving blocks, also called turf blocks, are ideal for such situations. They are set flush to the soil surface and protect soil from compaction. Grass can grow through the holes much like a regular lawn. A variety of types are available.

patches of grass may be caused by pockets of extremely sandy or clayey soil. Dig up the turf and analyze the soil as you would for a new lawn. If necessary, add organic matter and work it at least 6 inches into the soil.

Shade. Shade, especially heavy shade, poses problems for lawn grasses, which generally grow best in full sun. In too much shade, grasses may be anemic and prone to disease. Competition from shallow-rooted trees or shrubs can make the problem worse. If this is the case, replace the grass with a more shade-tolerant cultivar. Or replace the lawn with shade-loving ground covers.

Spills and other damage. Finally, determine if your own carelessness could have burned or harmed the grass. Did you spill gasoline, fertilizer, or an herbicide? If so, dig out the topsoil to a depth of 6 inches. Water the area well to leach the contaminant from the subsoil, then fill in the hole with fresh topsoil and replant.

REDUCING MAINTENANCE

Mowing, trimming, and edging the lawn can be time-consuming activities. While you are deciding on what to do about a problem lawn — or if you are simply tired of all that mowing — why not consider reducing the amount of time it takes to care for your lawn? Here are some tips to keep in mind. See Chapter 1 for more ideas on reducing maintenance.

Install edging strips. Installing edging strips helps keep grass from invading flower gardens and eliminates the need to edge beds manually. Plastic, aluminum, or steel edging strips are available. Plastic is easy to handle and cut, and it bends easily around curves. Aluminum is expensive, but is relatively easy to cut and won't rust. Steel is heavy, hard to cut, and it rusts, but it has a distinctive look many gardeners find appealing. None of these materials bends particularly well over a slope.

Use mulch and ground covers. Instead of letting lawn grass grow right up to every single tree and shrub in your yard, take time to reduce the number of obstacles you have to deal with. Use mulch and ground covers to create planting

The gentle, curving shape of this lawn makes it fast and easy to mow. Because of the wide brick edging strip, mowing and trimming can be accomplished in one step.

Laying Edging

Bricks, flagstones, or landscape timbers make excellent edging and mowing strips if they are laid flush with the soil surface. Lay them on a bed of sand and gravel that has been tamped down and watered in place. After you have positioned the edging strips, fill the gaps between pieces with sand.

islands that are easy to mow and trim around. A planting island could contain nothing more than a tree surrounded by mulch. Consider creating large islands with several trees, shrubs, and beds of ground covers, bulbs, and wildflowers. (Don't ever pile mulch against trees or shrubs. Keep it at least 4 inches away from the trunk and spread it to the tree's drip line.)

Installing Edging Strips

To install plastic, aluminum, or steel edging strips, dig a 4- to 5-inch trench and position the top edge of the strip just above the sod root zone. Backfill 1 to 2 inches below the top of the strip.

Other Edging Options

Pound-in edging comes in pieces that link together and can be pounded in place. They are ideal in spots where only a few feet of edging are needed.

Cover Slopes with Ground Covers

Reduce maintenance by planting hard-to-mow
slopes with ground covers instead of grass. Boards
pegged in place will help to decrease erosion.

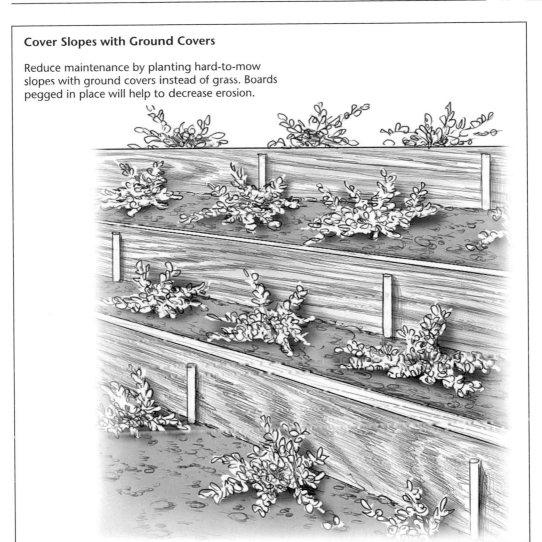

Fix tough-to-mow spots. Replace lawn on steep slopes with low-maintenance
ground covers to eliminate mowing problems and reduce the overall size of your
lawn. Fixing the hills and valleys in a bumpy lawn can also speed mowing chores
and eliminate problem spots in the process. Not only will you be able to skim
the mower along more quickly, you will eliminate scalped spots where your
mower cuts right to grass roots and valleys where the grass is always too long.

Fixing Low Spots

Step 1. To fix hills and valleys on a bumpy lawn, skim the grass off the site with a sharp spade. Roll it up and keep it moist until you replant it.

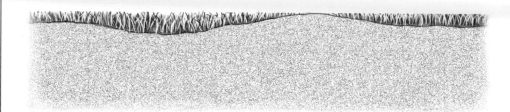

Step 2. Loosen the soil over the entire site, transferring excess soil to the low point in the process. Replace the sod, firm it in place, and keep it moist until the roots knit back into the soil.

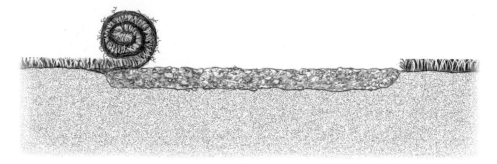

Simplify your lawn shape. The shape of your lawn will affect how fast you can mow it. A lawn with gentle curves and a rounded shape is easier and faster to mow than one with jagged, irregular edges. That's because you don't have to push the mower backwards and forwards to cut the grass and can simply sweep the mower quickly around the edges. An oval or round lawn is especially efficient because you can mow it easily in concentric circles. Mowing in concentric circles is faster than mowing in parallel rows, since you never have to pause to turn and realign the mower.

Plan for Efficient Mowing

Rounding off the shape of your lawn makes it easier and faster to mow because it eliminates corners and edges that you can only mow by pushing and pulling the mower back and forth repeatedly. With a rounded shape, you can skim around the lawn quickly and easily.

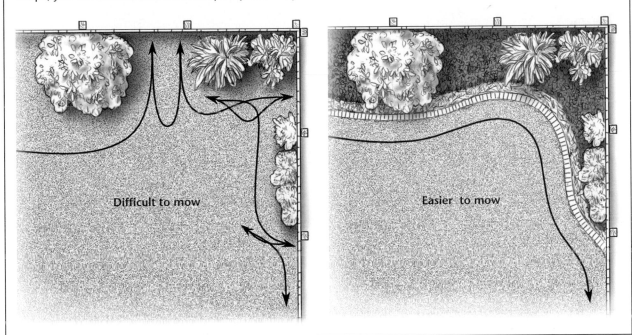

Difficult to mow

Easier to mow

DEALING WITH THATCH

To get rid of thatch and keep it from coming back, it helps to know something about how it is formed. Contrary to popular belief, grass clippings don't generally become thatch. In fact, in a properly managed lawn, clippings begin to decompose almost as soon as they hit the ground. (By tracing nitrogen isotopes, scientists found that nitrogen from clippings shows up in new growth of grass within a week.) In some situations, clippings can contribute to thatch — the clippings of bentgrass and red fescue, for example, are especially tough. If too much of the plant is cut at any one time, the long clippings that are left on the lawn will break down slowly, especially if the decomposition process is disrupted.

Thatch is primarily made up of the tougher parts of the grass plants — the stems, stolons, rhizomes, and roots, which are slower to break down than clippings. But in a well-maintained lawn, with healthy soil, these grass parts still will break down without forming thatch. That's because healthy soil is teeming with decomposers — microorganisms, such as fungi, bacteria, and actinomycetes, as well as insects and earthworms.

The presence of thatch is a sign that the decomposition system has broken down somehow. Most often poor maintenance practices cause the problem. If you mow too close, you will cut off stems and stolons and leave excessively long clippings. Overwatering may drown out the soil's decomposers and drive out earthworms. But most commonly thatch is caused by the excessive use of chemical fertilizers and pesticides. Chemical fertilizers tend to acidify soil and chase out earthworms, which prefer a neutral pH. Insecticides and fungicides both make the soil inhospitable to microorganisms and earthworms.

While a thin layer of thatch helps retain soil moisture and shields roots from extreme heat, a thick layer prevents water from reaching the grass roots and also harbors insects and diseases. If your lawn is plagued by thatch (a layer thicker than $1/2$ inch) you will have to develop a strategy to remove it and to keep it from coming back. Your plan will be a function of the size of your lawn and how much time and muscle you are willing to invest.

You can remove thatch manually with a heavy cavex, or thatch, rake. This tool has double-edged, crescent-shaped blades that slice through and pull up thatch. Pull the rake toward you, applying downward pressure; it will dislodge thatch and debris. Push the rake away from you to clean the thatch from the blades.

A thatch rake will do a good job on small lawns — up to 4,000 or 5,000 square feet. If your lawn is any larger, it pays to rent a gasoline-powered dethatcher, also known as a verticutter or vertimower. These machines operate like lawn mowers with vertical blades. As you guide the verticutter across the lawn, it slices through the thatch and lifts it to the surface where you can rake it away.

To prevent thatch from forming again, aerate the soil to reduce compaction and top-dress it to improve drainage and increase soil organic matter. Increasing soil organic matter also encourages earthworms, fungi, and other soil-dwellers, which decompose any thatch that does form.

Aerating and Top-dressing

Compacted soil starves grass roots of water and oxygen, causing thatch to build up. You can relieve compaction with another readily rented machine, a gasoline-powered core cultivator. This machine, which is suitable for aerating small lawns, pounds the lawn with hollow tubes that extract thin cores of soil a few inches long. Top-dressing with soil or compost then fills the holes with fresh medium for grass roots.

A core cultivator is a hand-and-foot-operated tool that looks something like a garden fork with two or four hollow tines. To use it, push the tines into the turf and then lift the tool to pull up cores of sod, soil, and thatch. As you push the cultivator down again at the next spot, the cores will pop out of the tines and fall onto the lawn. Continue across your lawn in this way until it is dotted with regularly spaced holes about 3 inches deep and half an inch in diameter.

After aerating the soil with a core cultivator, rake up the plugs and compost them, or simply pulverize them on the lawn. Top-dress to add organic matter to the soil and improve drainage.

After aerating, rake the soil cores up and compost them, or leave them in place and pulverize them with a rake. To finish the aerating job, top-dress your lawn by spreading a layer of topsoil, sand, or compost. This material seeps into the holes, where it improves the tilth, aeration, and drainage of the soil. Top-dressing with organic matter will increase soil microorganisms and earthworms, both of which help reduce thatch. Spread about ¾ cubic yard of topsoil for every 1,000 square feet of lawn, using a fertilizer spreader or broadcasting by hand. The best time to top-dress is in the fall. Although topsoil and sand are used most commonly for top-dressing, several other materials will work, including finely screened compost, ground seaweed, rotted sawdust, and well-rotted manure.

OVERSEEDING

A neglected, thin, weedy, disease- or pest-prone lawn can sometimes be restored with regular maintenance and overseeding. Try this technique if the area drains well and less than 25 percent of it is weeds. Since most new grasses are so vigorous that they will eventually crowd out old, weaker grass, overseeding is an excellent way to introduce improved grasses into your lawn. You can overseed with pest- and disease-resistant grasses (see "Plant Problem-Fighting Grasses" below), or a type that is more suited to the conditions of your yard, such as a

Plant Problem-Fighting Grasses

Today you can actually plant grass cultivars that resist pests and diseases. Cultivars of perennial ryegrass, tall fescue, and fine fescue are available that contain endophytes, which are fungi that occur naturally in grasses. The endophytes prevent a variety of leaf-eating lawn pests, including chinch bugs, sod webworms, and armyworms, from feeding, thus giving the grasses resistance to these pests.

Grass cultivars with resistance to diseases such as dollar spot and fusarium blight are also available. Ask your local extension agent or seed supplier for recommendations.

shade-tolerant grass, for example. If thatch or soil compaction contributed to the lawn's decline, remove the thatch and aerate before you overseed.

For best results, oversow in fall or early spring in the North and spring or early summer in the South. Before you sow, though, you have to make the existing lawn receptive to the new seed. First, mow the grass close, at half the normal mowing height — as low as $1/2$ inch, depending on the species of grass. Next, rake thoroughly and vigorously. Remove all the clippings and as much thatch as you can. Expose and rough up as much soil as possible, and pull up or hoe out all the weeds you find.

If you are reseeding an area larger than 1,000 square feet, the work will go faster if you rent a verticutter or a slice seeder. The verticutter resembles a lawn mower, but the blades are set vertically. It slices through the thatch and soil, exposing the soil and creating a good environment in which grass seed can germinate. Run the verticutter over the lawn in one direction, then run it back again in the opposite direction. A slice seeder is a more specialized piece of equipment that cuts through the sod and sows the seed at the same time.

Because you are not sowing the seed into bare soil, spread it more thickly — one and a half times the amount recommended on the package. For example, perennial ryegrass is usually planted at a rate of 4 to 6 pounds per 1,000 square feet; for overseeding, use 6 to 9 pounds. Use a drop spreader or spread the seed by hand, tossing it as you walk slowly over the lawn.

After sowing, rake the entire area lightly and top-dress the lawn with a thin layer of sand or topsoil. About $1/2$ cubic yard of soil should cover 1,000 square feet. Finally, water the area thoroughly, putting down at least 1 inch of water. Keep the reseeded area well watered, and stay off it until the grass has come up. Then don't mow until it has reached its maximum mowing height (2 to 4 inches, depending on the type of grass you planted).

RESEEDING AND RESODDING

To repair patches of damaged turf, you can either sow seed or use sod to cover the area. In either case, dig up the bad patch and as much as 6 inches of the surrounding turf, removing all turf and weeds. Then prepare the soil just as you would to sow a new lawn: Dig or till the soil to a depth of 6 inches, eliminating

To fix small patches of damaged lawn, remove damaged turf, loosen and improve the soil, and then seed or sod the spot with a grass that is compatible with the rest of your lawn.

Making Spot Repairs

Step 1. To prepare a damaged patch of lawn for reseeding or resodding, remove the damaged turf with a sharp spade. With a trowel or digging fork, loosen the soil and work in compost to improve the soil.

Step 2. You can seed the newly prepared soil or plant a small patch of sod. Treat the patch just as you would a new lawn. Keep the soil evenly moist and stay off of it until it is growing strongly.

any remaining weed and grass roots in the process. Then work compost or organic matter into the surface, rake the surface smooth, and water it thoroughly.

To resow, spread the seed evenly at the rate recommended on the package, then cover it with a thin (about ¼ inch) layer of topsoil, and water. Keep the soil surface evenly moist until the grass is at least 1 inch high. Also stay off the area and don't mow it until the grass has reached its maximum recommended height. You will get the best results if you sow during the preferred planting time for your area — fall or early spring in the North; late spring or early summer in the South.

If you are resodding, you can buy strips of sod at your local garden center. Make sure they will match the type of grass you already have growing. Or you can dig pieces of sod. Widening a flower bed or eliminating grass on a difficult-to-mow slope will yield sod you can use. Keep newly installed sod evenly moist until the roots grow into the soil.

REMOVING AN OLD LAWN

If your lawn is an unsightly, unhealthy quilt of bare patches, weeds, and anemic grass, it is probably best to tear it out and start over. In exchange for some hard work, you will get the opportunity to evaluate and amend the soil, fix drainage or grading problems, and wipe out weeds. Correcting underlying problems will give the new lawn an excellent chance for long-term health.

First you need to remove the existing vegetation, consisting of old sod, weeds, and thatch. There are several ways to remove an old lawn. You can rent a sod stripper (a machine about the size of a lawn mower that slices off the top layer of sod), or you can hire someone to do the job for you. Be prepared to lose some of your topsoil along with the sod. If your lawn is not too large and time is not of the essence, you can also mulch the vegetation to death. Cover the lawn with sheets of black plastic or newspaper, firmly anchored, and wait for the grass to die. Depending on the type of grass and the temperature, this can take from three to six weeks.

Once the existing lawn has been removed, prepare the site and soil as you would a new lawn, as outlined in Chapter 2.

Replacing Grass with Ground Covers

Step 1. To kill grass on a site that you would like to replant with ground covers, flowers, or other plants, cut the grass as low as possible. Then spread a thick layer of newspapers over the site. Anchor the newspapers with shovelsful of compost or chopped leaves if it is a windy day.

Step 2. Cover the newspapers with a mix of compost, grass clippings, and chopped leaves. Wait six to eight weeks, then loosen the soil on the site with a garden fork and sow grass seed. This technique can also be used to replace an existing lawn with new, improved grasses.

CHAPTER 5:

COPING WITH PESTS, DISEASES, AND WEEDS

A healthy, well cared for lawn is your best defense against most insects, diseases, and weeds. Proper mowing, watering, and fertilizing help prevent serious lawn problems, because they encourage lawn grass to grow vigorously, thus preventing problems from getting a foothold in the first place. Selecting the right grasses for your region is important in the fight against lawn problems, too. Lawn grasses recommended for your area will grow well in your climate instead of struggling against the prevailing heat and humidity, for example. Many also have resistance to pests or diseases common in your area.

If your lawn is attacked repeatedly by a variety of pests, diseases, and weeds, try to determine if there is an underlying condition that is causing the problem. Is the soil compacted? Are you mowing too low? Is the site shadier than you

---

Cultural problems like poor drainage or compacted soil are often responsible for lawns that are plagued by insects, diseases, and weeds. Improving the soil conditions and mowing and watering properly often will help reduce or eliminate future problems.

If you turn over a patch of grass and see more than three or four C-shaped larvae, you probably need to take steps to control them.

thought? Adjusting your routine maintenance practices may clear up the problem. Renovating is probably the best solution for a problem-plagued lawn. You can overseed with pest- or disease-resistant grasses (see "Plant Problem-Fighting Grasses" on page 72), or simply improve the soil conditions so the lawn grasses can grow more vigorously. See chapter 4, "Renovating a Lawn," on page 61 for more information.

Lawn diseases and insect problems can be difficult — if not impossible — for the average homeowner to diagnose. The truth is, a brown spot on the lawn may be caused by a number of different things — from insect feeding or fungal disease to dog damage. If you discover a problem area, look at it carefully, then read through the descriptions of damage for various common pests and diseases in this chapter. Look for signs of insects flying or hopping over the lawn when you walk across it. Pull at a piece of damaged turf and see if it comes up easily; damaged roots can indicate the presence of various root-feeding insects. Watch the problem to see if it begins to spread, and consider asking a lawn-care professional to come out and identify the cause. Many lawn-care companies offer diagnostic services to their customers. Your county agricultural extension agent may also be able to help. Be sure to ask for organic recommendations.

A GUIDE TO LAWN PESTS

Insects rarely cause serious problems in a healthy lawn. Occasionally, an infestation will require treatment, but before you spray or take any other action, do some scouting to make sure you know exactly what is causing the damage. Lawn pests may attack from either underground or above ground. Grubs, for example, attack from below. A common symptom of grub infestation is brown patches of lawn that are easy to pull up because the grass roots have been chewed off. See "Grubs" on page 87 for control options. To check for chinch bugs, cut both ends off a coffee can and press one end firmly into the grass. Fill the can with water. If chinch bugs are present, they will float to the surface of the water. If you find more than 20 bugs in the can, it is time to take action. See "Chinch Bugs" on page 84 for controls.

▪ Armyworms

DESCRIPTION: Armyworm larvae are pale green to greenish brown caterpillars with stripes on their sides and backs. Adults are pale gray-brown moths.

DAMAGE: Larvae chew grass blades to the crown of the plant, leaving bare, ragged patches in the lawn. They feed only at night and are a particular problem during cool, wet weather. In addition to lawn grasses, armyworms attack many different plants, including vegetables.

CONTROL: Apply parasitic nematodes to soil, or spray feeding larvae with BTK (*Bacillus thuringiensis* var. *kurstaki)* or neem. Dig up and replant dead areas of turf, then reseed with resistant lawn grasses that contain endophytes.

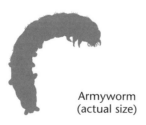

Armyworm
(actual size)

■ Billbugs

DESCRIPTION: Billbug larvae are small, white, legless larvae that look like grains of puffed rice with yellow heads. Adults are small brown or nearly black weevils (beetles with snouts).

DAMAGE: Larvae feed on grass stems starting in late spring, causing shoots to turn brown and die. They burrow under thatch and into the soil in summer and feed on roots and rhizomes. Infested lawns look drought-stressed.

CONTROL: Aerate the lawn, add organic matter, and water thoroughly. Reseed or overseed with resistant lawn grasses that contain endophytes. Spraying with rotenone will kill larvae and adults.

Billbug
(actual size)

Black turfgrass
ataenius
(actual size)

▪ Black turfgrass ataenius

DESCRIPTION: The larvae are tiny, soil-dwelling C-shaped grubs with brown heads. The adults are shiny black beetles, $1/4$ inch long, that are sometimes seen flying over the lawn during the warmest part of the day.

DAMAGE: The adults chew grass roots and underground rhizomes, causing brown patches of lawn that are easy to pull up.

CONTROL: Apply parasitic nematodes to the soil or spray with pyrethrin to control the larvae. See also "Grubs" on page 87 for another control option.

▪ Chinch bugs

DESCRIPTION: Chinch bug larvae are red with a white stripe and smaller than a pinhead when they hatch. When mature, they are $1/6$ inch long and black with white wings. Adults have a foul odor when crushed — or when infested turf is walked on.

DAMAGE: These pests suck the sap from grass at all stages of development, causing rounded patches of turf to turn yellow and die. The dying patches steadily enlarge.

CONTROL: Keep the lawn well watered, since these pests prefer hot, sunny conditions. Reseed or overseed with resistant lawn grasses that contain endophytes. Dust the lawn with sabadilla.

Chinch bug
(actual size)

Cutworm
(actual size)

▪ Cutworms

DESCRIPTION: Cutworms are plump, smooth, brown, gray, or green, 1-inch caterpillars. They curl up when disturbed in the soil. Adults are brown or grayish moths.

DAMAGE: Cutworms are primarily a problem on newly seeded lawns, and then only if infestations are severe. They chew through grass blades near the soil line. The larvae are active only at night and are most troublesome in spring. Birds scratching for these pests also damage seedlings.

CONTROL: If infestations are severe, spray the lawn with pyrethrin in early evening, just as the cutworms are emerging. Applying predatory nematodes to the soil will also help control cutworms.

Fire ant
(actual size)

■ Fire Ants

DESCRIPTION: These tiny yellowish, reddish, or blackish ants build
large mounds in the lawn.

DAMAGE: The mounds are unsightly and the ants themselves are dangerous;
they have a painful sting and attack humans and animals who step on their
mounds.

CONTROL: Insect growth regulators, which kill colonies slowly by preventing
normal development, are available. Citrus oil products also have been shown to
control these pests.

■ Grasshoppers

DESCRIPTION: Elongated yellow, green, or brown insects with long hind legs
and hard outer covering.

DAMAGE: Grasshoppers feed on and consume aboveground portions of lawn
grasses and other plants. A few on the lawn will not do any lasting harm.

CONTROL: Handpick the pests; watering the lawn before picking helps make
them easier to catch. If problems are significant every year,
inoculate the soil with *Nosema locustae*,
a disease-causing spore.

Grasshopper
(actual size)

■ Grubs

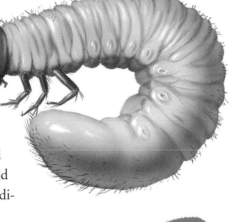

DESCRIPTION: Grubs are plump, whitish, C-shaped or wormlike creatures, from ¹/₂ inch to 1¹/₂ inches long. They often have dark heads. Grubs are the larvae of various beetles, including Japanese beetles and June beetles.

DAMAGE: Grubs feed on grass roots, damaging patches of turf so that they're easy to pull up. Severe infestations can kill large patches. Damage is usually most serious during fall and spring. Skunks, birds, and moles digging in your yard often indicate grub infestations.

CONTROL: Milky disease is a biological control that attacks grubs. Use a fertilizer spreader to apply the spores evenly over your lawn. It may take several seasons to produce a noticeable effect, but once the spores build up, they will provide long-term control. For faster results, apply parasitic nematodes to affected areas.

Grub
(actual size)

■ Leafhoppers

DESCRIPTION: Adult leafhoppers are small, greenish, wedge-shaped, soft-bodied insects that hop quickly across the lawn when disturbed.

DAMAGE: Both leafhopper adults and their similar-looking nymphs feed on grass blades. They suck plant juices, causing dried-out blades and pale whitish areas. If you look closely, you can see tiny white spots where they have been feeding.

CONTROL: Leafhoppers are not a major problem on established lawns but can do considerable damage to a newly seeded one. Dust serious infestations with pyrethrin.

Leafhopper
(actual size)

■ Mites

DESCRIPTION: Adult mites are very tiny white- or rust-colored spiderlike pests that you need a hand lens to see. Some mites spin fine webs around leaves or between leaves and stems.

DAMAGE: Mites suck plant juices from leaves, producing a light-colored stippling on leaf surfaces. Serious infestations will cause patches of thin brown grass.

CONTROL: Mites thrive in hot, dry conditions, so sprinkling the lawn frequently can reduce infestations. Spray serious infestations with insecticidal soap, neem, or pyrethrin.

Mite
(actual
size)

Mole cricket
(actual size)

■ Mole crickets

DESCRIPTION: Adults are large brownish insects that are 1 to 1½ inches long. They are covered with many short hairs and have flattened front feet that are well adapted to digging in the soil. Nymphs are similar but smaller.

DAMAGE: Mole crickets tunnel under lawn grasses and feed on roots, causing irregular brown or dead patches. They may also feed on the roots of garden plants. Mole crickets are a problem in southern gardens. Damage is most serious during warm, moist weather.

CONTROL: Apply a solution of parasitic nematodes to the soil in infested areas, then water thoroughly.

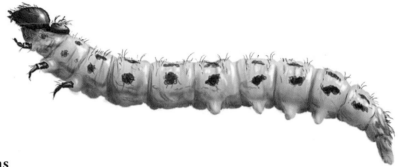

■ Sod webworms

DESCRIPTION: Sod webworms are $1/2$- to 1-inch-long gray, cream, or light brown caterpillars with dark-spotted backs. Adults are whitish or gray moths that fly in a zigzag pattern.

DAMAGE: Larvae feed on the blades of grass plants, producing small, irregular brown or dead patches. They also produce silken tunnels in the ground. Damage is most serious in mid- to late summer, especially during hot, dry conditions. Sod webworms attack most turf grasses but are particularly attracted to bentgrasses and bluegrasses.

CONTROL: Drenching infested areas with BTK *(Bacillus thuringiensis* var. *kurstaki)* or parasitic nematodes may help control these pests. If sod webworms are a problem every year, consider overseeding or reseeding with endophyte-containing turfgrass cultivars.

Sod webworm
(actual size)

MANAGING LAWN DISEASES

Disease diagnosis and cure are the most mysterious aspects of lawn care. There are scores of common grass diseases, and all but one (St. Augustine decline virus) are caused by fungi. Many have symptoms so similar that only a plant pathologist can make a definitive identification. Some, however, are easy to spot. Fortunately, there are some general preventive steps anyone can take to keep a lawn free of disease.

Trying to grow the wrong type of grass in the wrong place is what makes a lawn most susceptible to disease. Growing a grass unsuitable for your region — a warm-season grass in a cool area, a water-loving grass in a dry climate, or a delicate grass in a heavily trafficked area — will cause stress to the grass, and stress invites disease. If you have a disease problem, look first at the type of grass and the cultivar you're growing. If you need to replace it, take heart: New grass cultivars are likely to be much more disease-resistant. From 'Midnight' Kentucky bluegrass, which resists leafspot and melting out, to 'Reliant' fine fescue, which resists powdery mildew, there is a type and cultivar immune to nearly every disease. If you are shopping for grass, it pays to go with the new, named cultivars that carry disease resistance. Ask your local cooperative extension service or garden center for the best new cultivars for your area.

Although disease-causing fungi are always present in the soil, they are not always active enough to cause damage; other factors may hold them in check, especially in a healthy, vigorous lawn. Most outbreaks are triggered by poor cultural practices. Providing too much or too little fertilizer and/or water can invite disease problems, as can improper mowing. See "A Guide to Common Lawn Diseases" on page 92 for a list of diseases, symptoms, and cultural conditions that promote them.

Excessive use of insecticides, herbicides, and even fungicides also can lead to outbreaks. Countless studies have shown that a fungicide applied to cure one disease opens the gates for others. The reason is that fungicides (and to some degree herbicides and insecticides too) damage beneficial organisms in the soil. Healthy soil is teeming with fungi, bacteria, and actinomycetes that work to keep the pathogens in check. For a disease-free lawn, you should seek to keep the soil alive

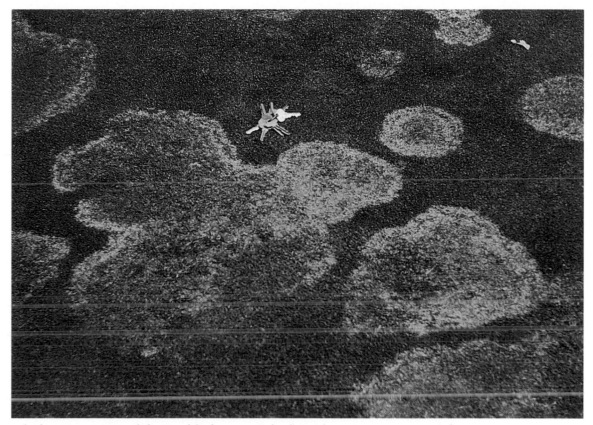

The best way to control diseases like brown patch, shown here, is to grow a type of grass that is suitable for your region. Adding organic matter by aerating and top-dressing will improve drainage and discourage fungal diseases from getting a foothold. You can also overseed a lawn with one of the new disease-resistant lawn grasses.

with these little fighters. Cutting down on chemicals will help. You can also increase the life of the soil by fertilizing or top-dressing with manure or compost. If your lawn looks poor, don't blame disease right off the bat. While diseases generally occur as patches, rings, or spots of discolored grass, there can be other causes of such symptoms, including dog damage, herbicide burning, spilled gasoline or other chemicals, poor drainage, and compacted soils. Make sure you check for all of these first.

If you can find no other probable cause, consult a professional — your extension agent, a local garden center, or a lawn-care service representative that can provide recommendations for organic controls. The expert will need the answers to the following questions in order to make a diagnosis: What type of grass is affected? What are the symptoms and when did they first appear? Have the symptoms changed over time? If so, how? Has the area changed shape or grown larger? Do the grass blades in the area looked striped or show patterns or lesions? Is the area in sun or shade? The more accurate and complete your answers, the better the chance that the expert will make a correct diagnosis and recommend the proper cure.

Here is a list of some common grass diseases along with notes on what they look like and cultural conditions that promote them.

A Guide to Common Lawn Diseases

▪ Brown patch

DESCRIPTION: Dark or water-soaked patches that turn brown. Brown patch generally appears in hot, humid weather (between 80° and 85°F). Patches can range from a few inches to several feet in diameter.

CULTURAL CONTROLS: This disease is most common on heavily fertilized lawns as well as lawns growing in poorly drained soil. Adding organic matter to the soil by top-dressing with compost or aerating and then top-dressing will improve drainage.

▪ Dollar spot

DESCRIPTION: Round, bleached-out spots about the size of a silver dollar. The spots enlarge and eventually overlap.

CULTURAL CONTROLS: Dollar spot attacks lawns growing in dry soil that is low in nitrogen and most commonly appears when days are warm and nights are cool. Regular watering and feeding, especially with nitrogen, will help combat it.

- ## Fusarium blight

DESCRIPTION: Patches 2 to 6 inches in diameter that turn red-brown then tan and yellow. Grass roots and crowns are also rotted.

CULTURAL CONTROLS: This disease is a problem in hot, humid, summer weather on lawns that are under stress. Adequate watering, feeding, and good general care help prevent it.

- ## Melting out

DESCRIPTION: Tan spots with reddish brown borders, followed by rotting stems, crowns, and roots.

CULTURAL CONTROLS: Melting out is a disease of cool, wet weather. Watering deeply and infrequently in hot weather, avoiding heavy applications of fertilizer, and dethatching will all help prevent it. Plant or overseed with resistant grass cultivars.

- ## Powdery mildew

DESCRIPTION: Small patches of white or gray fungus on grass blades.

CULTURAL CONTROLS: Powdery mildew is primarily a problem on Kentucky bluegrass, especially in shady areas, and is most prevalent in cool, wet weather and on overfertilized lawns. Plant or overseed with resistant grass cultivars; plant shade-tolerant grasses in shady areas. Cut back on fertilizer and water only in the morning.

- ## Pythium blight

DESCRIPTION: Circular spots of dark, water-soaked grass growing together to form large, irregular clusters.

CULTURAL CONTROLS: This is a fast-spreading disease that is difficult to stop, so prevention is important. Test soil pH and adjust it to between 6 and 7. Dethatch and avoid watering in the evening.

■ **Red thread**

DESCRIPTION: Red threads of fungus that extend from the grass blades. Grass is often affected in patches up to 2 feet in diameter.

CULTURAL CONTROLS: Cool, wet weather promotes this disease. Regular mowing and deep watering help prevent it, as does providing adequate nitrogen.

■ **Rust**

DESCRIPTION: Rust-colored spores on grass blades.

CULTURAL CONTROLS: Drought-stressed, nutrient-starved grasses and hot, dry weather all promote rust outbreaks. Adequate watering, feeding, and good general care help prevent it. Plant or overseed with resistant grass cultivars.

■ **Stripe smut**

DESCRIPTION: Yellow or brown grass with dark stripes on the blades. Infected blades eventually dry out and die.

CULTURAL CONTROLS: Stripe smut attacks weak turf in cool weather. Adequate watering, feeding, and good general care help prevent it. Plant or overseed with resistant grass cultivars.

■ **Summer patch**

DESCRIPTION: Patches of dead grass mixed with live plants.

CULTURAL CONTROLS: This disease is a problem in hot, humid, summer weather on lawns that are under stress. Adequate watering, feeding, and good general care help prevent it. Plant or overseed with resistant grass cultivars.

CONTROLLING WEEDS

The best defense against weeds is a vigorous lawn. If your lawn is thick and healthy, weeds won't have room to make any inroads. Many weed infestations are caused by easy-to-correct problems, such as too much fertilizer or compacted soil, that prevent the grass from growing vigorously enough to conquer the weeds. Even how and when you mow can have a major effect. A high-growing lawn will shade low-growing weeds and weaken them. Shade will also discourage weed seeds from germinating.

When it comes time to control weeds, many gardeners automatically reach for the herbicide. People who carefully hand-weed their vegetable gardens and flower borders never think of hand-weeding their lawns too. But it can be done. Just take care to remove as much of the weed and its root as possible, while disturbing as little of the lawn as you can. With a long-handled lawn weeding tool, you can even avoid crawling around on your hands and knees.

Remember that weeds are vigorous invaders that will quickly colonize a bare spot on the lawn. So it's a good idea to carry around a bag of topsoil and some grass seed as you weed. When a weed comes out, fill in the divot with soil and sprinkle some seeds.

Here is a list of some common lawn weeds along with notes on the controls and the cultural conditions that promote them.

Weed Effectively

The right tools will help you weed effectively. Use a dandelion fork to probe into the soil and dig out deep-rooted weeds so they won't return.

▪ Annual bluegrass

DESCRIPTION: Annual bluegrass *(Poa annua)* is a low-growing relative of Kentucky bluegrass that sets seeds, then turns brown and dies in hot summer weather. It prefers moist, compacted soil.

CONTROL: Mow higher so taller grasses will shade it out. Aerate the soil to eliminate compacted conditions. Pick up seed heads and dispose of them. Dig out plants and replant with perennial lawn grasses.

■ Bermudagrass

DESCRIPTION: An easy-care turfgrass in the South, Bermudagrass *(Cynodon dactylon)* can spread rapidly by rhizomes and stolons and can become very invasive. It turns brown after frost and can be invaded by weeds in winter.

CONTROL: Dig up clumps and reseed or resod the areas with more favored grasses.

■ Broadleaf plantain

DESCRIPTION: Broadleaf plantain *(Plantago major)* is a perennial weed that reproduces by seed. It grows in low rosettes of oval green leaves with prominent veins on the undersides of the foliage. During summer and early fall, narrow 4- to 12-inch spikes of small green flowers arise from the center of the rosettes.

CONTROL: Pull plants or cut them off at soil level every week or two. Broadleaf plantain thrives in heavy, compacted soil, so aerate the site and add organic matter to loosen the soil; this will discourage the weed from returning.

▪ Common chickweed

DESCRIPTION: Common chickweed *(Stellaria media)* is an annual weed that spreads mainly by seed. It forms dense mats of many-branched, trailing or weakly upright stems that root where they touch the soil. Plants may be up to 12 inches tall but are often much lower. The stems bear pairs of small oval leaves with pointed tips and tiny white flowers from early spring through fall.

CONTROL: Hoe or pull seedlings; resow or sod bare patches to prevent more seeds from sprouting. Pull, cut, or mow larger plants before they flower and set seed.

▪ Crabgrasses

DESCRIPTION: Crabgrasses (*Digitaria* spp.) are grassy, annual weeds that spread by seed. Branching, thick, spreading stems carry coarse blue-green to purplish leaf blades that may be smooth or hairy. From summer into fall, plants are topped with narrow, fingerlike spikes of inconspicuous florets. Plants may grow up to 3 feet tall but adapt quickly to whatever mowing height you use.

CONTROL: Pull or dig plants before they set seed. In lawns, discourage crabgrass from returning by taking steps to improve lawn vigor. Fertilize and lime as needed, and water deeply only when the grass shows signs of wilting. Avoid mowing too low — 2 inches is fine for most lawns. Thick, healthy turf will shade out crabgrass and discourage seeds from sprouting.

■ Dallisgrass

DESCRIPTION: Dallisgrass *(Paspalum dilatatum)* is a perennial grass that produces clumps of yellow-green leaves, each with a white margin. It spreads by rhizomes and seed. Plants can reach 5 feet, but are considerably shorter in mown areas. They begin growing in early spring, before most lawn grasses, and form unattractive, tall clumps in the lawn. Dallisgrass is generally found in the southern portions of the country and thrives in fertile, well-watered turf.

CONTROL: Dig clumps up, taking care to get as many of the short rhizomes as possible. Sod or reseed the patches as you weed. Let plants dry thoroughly before composting them. Or, cut plants to the ground and smother them with cardboard, left in place for two months or more. Avoid spring feeding and watering.

■ Dandelion

DESCRIPTION: Dandelion *(Taraxacum officinale)* is a perennial weed that spreads mainly by seed. Rosettes of serrated or straight-edged leaves grow from thick taproots with branching crowns. Each 2- to 12-inch hollow flower stem is topped with a 1- to 2-inch-wide bloom that is packed with narrow, strap-shaped, yellow petals. These flowers mature into puffy white seed heads. Plants may bloom any time from spring to frost, or year-round in warm areas.

CONTROL: Dig plants as soon as you spot them, getting as much of the taproot as possible, or cut plants to the ground. Cut regrowth every week or two, or mulch with cardboard or a thick layer of newspapers for one growing season.

▪ Foxtails

DESCRIPTION: Foxtails (*Setaria* spp.) are grassy, annual weeds that reproduce by seed. The upright or creeping stems branch at the base and bear flat green leaf blades. From summer into fall, the stems are topped with hairy greenish to yellowish spikes that may be upright or nodding. Plants may grow up to 3 feet tall but can grow much lower in mowed areas.

CONTROL: Hoe or pull seedlings; mulch bare soil to prevent more seeds from sprouting. Dig out older plants or cut them to the ground every week or two until no new sprouts appear.

■ Goosegrass

DESCRIPTION: Goosegrass *(Eleusine indica)* resembles crabgrass but is larger and darker green in color. These annuals can reach 2 feet in unmowed areas, but adapt readily to any height in a lawn. Plants produce seedheads with three or more narrow spikes at the top. Goosegrass will grow in nearly any soil, but is especially able to colonize lawns on compacted, poorly drained soil. Mowing too low and shallow, and frequent watering are also favorable conditions for goosegrass.

CONTROL: Pull or dig up plants in spring and summer to prevent self-seeding. Aerating or topdressing soil, mowing as high as possible, and watering only when necessary will also discourage goosegrass.

■ Ground ivy

DESCRIPTION: Ground ivy *(Glechoma hederacea)* is a perennial weed that reproduces by seed and by creeping stems that root as they spread. Plants are usually less than 3 inches tall and have square stems with pairs of bright green, rounded leaves with scalloped edges. Small purplish flowers bloom along the stems in spring. Plants have a minty odor when crushed.

CONTROL: Pull stems and roots as soon as you notice the plants; repeat every week or two to control regrowth. Regular fertilizing and aerating can improve lawn vigor and discourage the weed from returning. To reclaim heavily infested areas, pull or mow plants, then mulch with cardboard or a thick layer of newspapers for at least one growing season.

■ Henbit

DESCRIPTION: Henbit *(Lamium amplexicaule)* is an annual or biennial weed that reproduces mainly by seed. The square sprawling stems root where they touch the soil; upright branches to 1 foot tall arise from the main stems. The hairy, rounded, scalloped leaves are borne in pairs; the bases of the upper leaves clasp the stem. Clusters of pinkish to purple flowers appear near the tops of the stems in spring or fall.

CONTROL: Hoe or pull seedlings; mulch bare soil to discourage more seeds from germinating. Dig or pull larger plants before they set seed.

■ Nimblewill

DESCRIPTION: Nimblewill *(Muhlenbergia schreiberi)* is a grassy perennial weed that reproduces mainly by seed. The slender, branching stems may also root at the lower leaf joints; they tend to grow more upright toward the tips, with flat and slender leaf blades. In fall, the stems are topped with thin spikes of inconspicuous green florets that turn reddish brown as they mature. Plants may reach 2 feet tall but can grow lower in mowed areas.

CONTROL: Dig out plants and their roots, or hoe or cut stems to the ground. Repeat every week or two to control regrowth, or mulch with cardboard or a thick layer of newspapers for one growing season.

▪ Prostrate knotweed

DESCRIPTION: Prostrate knotweed *(Polygonum aviculare)* is an annual weed that reproduces by seed. The branched stems generally creep along the ground but may turn upward at the ends; plants are usually no more than 12 inches tall. The stems bear lance-shaped to oblong, pointed, blue-green leaves that turn reddish brown after a killing frost. Tiny white or yellowish flowers bloom along the stems from midsummer through fall.

CONTROL: Hoe or pull seedlings; mulch bare soil to prevent more seeds from sprouting. Pull or cut older plants to the ground before they set seed, being sure to get the crown (where the stems join the roots). Prostrate knotweed thrives in compacted, high-traffic areas; prevent its return by adding organic matter to loosen the soil and by aerating lawn areas yearly.

■ Prostrate spurge

DESCRIPTION: Prostrate spurge *(Euphorbia maculata)* is an annual weed that reproduces by seed. The slender reddish or purplish stems branch freely; they may creep or turn upright at the tips. Plants form broad mats that are normally less than 6 inches tall. The greenish leaves are oblong to oval and usually have a purple-brown blotch on the top. Leaves, stems, and roots exude a milky sap when broken. Inconspicuous flowers bloom in clusters along stems from summer into fall.

CONTROL: Hoe, pull, or dig out plants before they set seed. Mulch bare soil to prevent more seeds from sprouting.

▪ Purslane

DESCRIPTION: Common purslane *(Portulaca oleracea)* is an annual that produces sprawling stems with fleshy, rounded leaves. The stems root at the joints, aiding the plant's spread. Plants thrive in dry conditions and will set seed from spring to fall, although they generally stop during the hottest part of the summer.

CONTROL: Dig or pull up plants anytime during the season, taking care to remove all stem segments. (Both leaves and stems are edible; you can add them to salads. Aerating the soil and watering regularly also help control purslane.

■ Quackgrass

DESCRIPTION: Quackgrass *(Agropyron repens)* is a grassy, perennial weed that reproduces by seeds and fast-creeping roots (rhizomes). The narrow blue-green leaves are soft and flat; their bases clasp the stem. Narrow spikes of green florets bloom atop the stems from summer into early fall. Plants may reach 4 feet tall but can grow lower in mowed areas.

CONTROL: Dig out the roots and slender, pointed rhizomes as thoroughly as possible; be on the lookout for new shoots from missed roots. Or hoe or cut plants to the ground every week or two until no new shoots appear. In severely infested areas, cut or mow plants, then mulch with cardboard or a thick layer of newspapers for at least one growing season.

■ Wild garlic

DESCRIPTION: Wild garlic *(Allium vineale)* is a perennial weed that reproduces by seed and bulblets. Its underground bulbs produce stiff, upright, leafy stems. The slender leaves taper at the tip and wrap around the stem at the base. Stems may be topped with a rounded cluster of greenish to purplish small flowers or tiny bulblets in late spring to early summer. Wild garlic can reach 3 feet tall but is lower in mowed areas. All parts of the plant have a strong onion or garlic odor when crushed.

CONTROL: Dig clumps, being sure to get as many of the bulbs as possible. Or cut plants to the ground every week or two, until no new growth appears. In heavily infested areas, cut or mow plants, then mulch with cardboard or a thick layer of newspapers for at least one growing season.

▪ Yellow nutsedge

DESCRIPTION: Yellow nutsedge *(Cyperus esculentus)* is a perennial weed that reproduces by seed and by thin creeping stems tipped with hard, small tubers. The upright, three-sided, 1-foot stems bear pale green grasslike leaves; the leaf bases wrap around the stems. Plants are topped with loosely branched, scaly, golden brown spikes from summer into fall.

CONTROL: Pull or cut down plants as soon as you see them. Keep removing new shoots every week or two until no more sprouts appear; persistence is the key. In severely infested areas, cut or mow plants, then mulch with cardboard or a thick layer of newspapers for at least one growing season.

Hardiness Zone Map

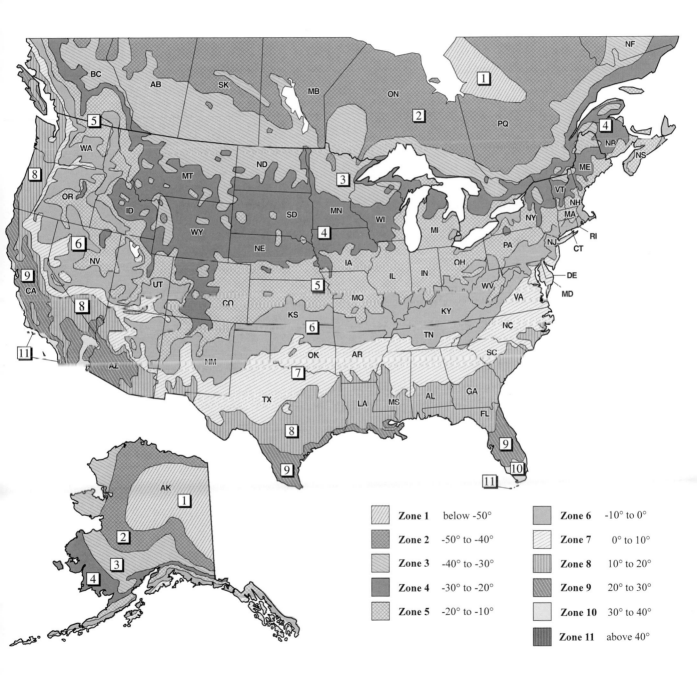

Zone 1	below -50°	Zone 6	-10° to 0°
Zone 2	-50° to -40°	Zone 7	0° to 10°
Zone 3	-40° to -30°	Zone 8	10° to 20°
Zone 4	-30° to -20°	Zone 9	20° to 30°
Zone 5	-20° to -10°	Zone 10	30° to 40°
		Zone 11	above 40°

Photo Credits

INDEX

Achillea spp., 22
Aerating, 71–72
Agricultural extension agents,
    81, 92
Agropyron repens, 111
Ajuga, 8, 16
Allium vineale, 112
Alternatives to lawn grass, 16, 17,
    18–21, 22–23, 67
Amendments for soil, 36–37
Annual bluegrass (*Poa annua*),
    27, 96
Annual ryegrass, 27, 28, 50
Ants, fire, 86
Armyworms, 82

Bacillus thuringiensis var. *kurstaki,*
    82, 89
Bahiagrass, 29, 49, 50
Beetles
    black turfgrass ataenius, 84
    grubs, 87
Bentgrass
    description of, 28
    fertilizing of, 57
    in lawn-grass seed, 27
    pest problems with, 89
    thatch problems with, 69
Bermudagrass (*Cynodon dactylon*)
    description of, 28, 29, 53, 97
    maintenance of, 49, 57
    planting of, 44, 45
    zones for, 26
Billbugs, 83
Black turfgrass ataenius, 84
Blue gramma grass
    description of, 20, 28, 29, 53
    mowing of, 49

    zones for, 26
Bluegrass, annual (*Poa annua*), 27,
    96
Bluegrass, Kentucky
    cultivars of, 41, 90
    description of, 28, 32
    diseases of, 93
    maintenance of, 49, 57
    zones for, 26
Bluegrass, rough (*Poa trivalis*), 27
Bluegrasses, pest problems
    with, 89
Broadcast seeders, 41–42, 41
Broadleaf plantain (*Plantago
    major*), 98
Brown patch, 91, 92
BTK (*Bacillus thuringiensis* var.
    kurstaki) , 82, 89
Budget considerations in
    planning, 4, 23, 27, 39, 45
Buffalograss
    description of, 20, 28, 30, 53
    maintenance of, 49, 57
    zones for, 26
Bulb planters, 7, 23
Bulbs, 6–7
Bumpy lawn, repair of, 67, 68
Bunchgrasses, 28

Cardboard collars for pest
    control, 85
Carpetgrass, 30, 49
Caterpillars
    armyworms, 82
    cutworms, 85
    sod webworms, 89
Cavex (thatch rake), 70
Centipedegrass

description of, 30–31
    maintenance of, 49
    planting of, 45
    zones for, 26
Chemical fertilizers, 70
Chewings fescue, 32
Chickweed, common (*Stellaria
    media*), 99
Chinch bugs, 81, 84–85
Citrus oil products, 86
Clay soil
    corrections for, 36–37
    grasses for, 30
Clippings. *See* Grass clippings
Coarse-bladed grasses, 28
Common chickweed (*Stellaria
    media*), 99
Compaction of soil, 34, 71, 73.
    See also Mulched areas;
    Paving stones; Traffic-
    tolerant grasses
Compost. *See* Organic matter
Cool-season grasses. *See also names
    of specific grasses*
    description of, 28, 32–33
    fertilizing of, 55
    mowing of, 49
    planting of, 40
Core cultivators, 71
Coreopsis, 22
Cotoneasters, low-growing, 16
Crabgrasses (*Digitaria* spp.), 100
Crested wheatgrass, 26
Crickets, mole, 88–89
Cultivars, 41, 72, 89, 90
Cutworms, 85
Cynodon dactylon. See
    Bermudagrass
Cyperus esculentus, 113

Dallisgrass *(Paspalum dilatatum)*, 101
Dandelion *(Taraxacum officinale)*, 102
Dandelion forks, 95
Decking, ground-level, 14, 21
Design considerations in lawn planning, 4–12
Dethatchers, 70
Diagnosing lawn problems, 62–64, 79–81
Digitaria spp., 100
Disease-resistant grasses, 72, 90
  carpetgrass, 30, 49
  centipedegrass, 26, 30–31, 45, 49
  fine fescues, 29, 32, 49, 57, 72, 90
  Kentucky bluegrass, 26, 28, 32, 49, 57, 90, 93
  perennial ryegrass, 26, 28, 29, 33, 49, 72, 73
  tall fescue, 20, 26, 28, 33, 62, 72
Diseases
  causes of, 90–92
  description of, 92–94
Dollar spot, 92
Dormancy, 53
Drainage of soil, 36, 62
Drop spreaders, 57
Drought-tolerant grasses, 1, 18–21, 28
  Bermudagrass, 26, 28, 29, 44, 45, 49, 53, 57, 97
  blue gramma grass, 20, 26, 28, 29, 49, 53
  buffalograss, 20, 26, 28, 30, 49, 53, 57
  fine fescues, 29, 32, 49, 57, 72
  zoysiagrass, 26, 28, 31, 44, 45, 49

Earthworms, 70
Edging, 9, 57–59

Edging strips, 20, 57–58, 59, 64, 65, 66
Edging tools, 59
Eleusine indica, 104
English ivy, 8, 16
Equipment. *See* Tools
'Estate' Kentucky bluegrass, 41
Euphorbia maculata, 109
Evening primroses (*Oenothera* spp.), 22

Fertilizer spreaders, 57, 72
Fertilizers
  application of, 37, 53–57
  lawn damage from, 54, 64
  and thatch development, 70
  types of, 48, 54–55 (table), 57
Fescues, 28, 40
  chewings, 32
  fine, 29, 32, 49, 57, 72
  red, 20, 26, 32, 69
  'Reliant' fine, 90
  tall, 20, 26, 28, 33, 49, 62, 72
Fine fescue, 29, 32, 49, 57, 72, 90
Fine-bladed grasses, 27–28
Fire ants, 86
Foxtails (*Setaria* spp.), 103
Fungicides, 90
Fusarium blight, 93

Gaillardia, 22
Garlic, wild *(Allium vineale),* 112
Gasoline, lawn damage from, 64
Glechoma hederacea, 105
Goosegrass *(Eleusine indica),* 104
Grading soil, 33–36. *See also* Slopes
Gramma grass. *See* Blue gramma grass; Sideoats gramma grass
Grass clippings
  mulching of, 48, 50

and thatch development, 69–70
  use of, 48
Grass seed. *See* Seed, buying of; Seeding
Grass shears, 57
Grasses. *See also names of specific grasses*
  selection of, 25–28
  types of, 29–33
  zone map for, 26
Grasshoppers, 86
Ground covers, 18
  as lawn alternatives, 3, 16, 18, 21, 67
  as lawn complements, 8
  to reduce lawn maintenance, 64–66
Ground ivy *(Glechoma hederacea),* 105
Grubs, 81, 87; of black turfgrass ataenius, 84

Hardiness zone map, USDA, 115
Heat-tolerant grasses
  perennial ryegrass, 26, 28, 29, 33, 49, 72, 73
  tall fescue, 20, 26, 28, 33, 62, 72
Henbit *(Lamium amplexicaule),* 106
Herbicides, lawn damage from, 64, 90. *See also* Weeds, control of
High-traffic areas. *See* Compaction of soil; Mulched areas; Paving stones; Traffic-tolerant grasses
Hoes, 45

Insect growth regulators, 86
Insecticidal soap, 88
Insecticides. *See* Pesticides

Insect-resistant grasses, 72
    carpetgrass, 30, 49
    centipedegrass, 26, 30–31,
        45, 49
    fine fescues, 29, 32, 49, 57, 72
    perennial ryegrass, 26, 28, 29,
        33, 49, 72, 73
    St. Augustine grass, 26, 28, 31,
        44, 45, 49, 50
    tall fescue, 20, 26, 28, 33,
        62, 72
Irrigation. *See* Watering
Ivy, English, 8, 16. *See also*
    Ground ivy

Japanese beetles, 87
June beetles, 87
Junipers, 8, 16

Kentucky bluegrass. *See* Bluegrass,
    Kentucky
Knotweed, prostrate *(Polygonum
    aviculare),* 108

Lamium amplexicaule, 106
Lawn Institute, 27
Lawn rollers, 43
Lawns
    alternatives to, 16, 17, 18–21,
        22–23, 67
    amount of, 4
    damage to, 62–64
    diseases of, 90–94
    function of, 4
    grass types for, 25–28
    maintenance of, 4, 12–16,
        47–59, 64–68, 70, 79
    pest control and, 81–89
    planning of, 3–23
    planting of, 25–45
    removal of, 76, 77
    renovation of, 61–77
    weeds of, 95–113

Leafhoppers, 87
Leaves, raking of, 56
Liriope, 16
Low-maintenance lawns. *See*
    Maintenance

Maintenance, 47–59
    consideration of in lawn
        planning, 3–4, 12–16, 22
    reduction of, 64–68
    and thatch development, 70
    troubleshooting with, 79
    of wildflower meadows and
        prairies, 22–23
Manure. *See* Organic matter
Meadows, wildflower, 22–23
Melting out, 93
'Merit' Kentucky bluegrass, 41
'Midnight' Kentucky bluegrass, 90
Milky disease, 87
Mites, 88
Mole crickets, 88–89
Moths
    armyworms, 82
    cutworms, 85
    sod webworms, 89
Mowers, selection of, 48, 49–50
Mowing, 12–16, 47–50, 66–69
Muhlenbergia schreiberi, 107
Mulched areas
    as lawn alternative, 12, 16, 21
    placement of, 14
    to reduce lawn maintenance,
        58, 64–66
Mulching mowers, 48, 49–50

Native grasses, as lawn
    alternatives, 18–20, 22
Neem, 82, 88
Nematodes, parasitic, 82, 84, 85,
    87, 89
Nimblewill *(Muhlenbergia
    schreiberi),* 107
Northern U.S.

dormant period in, 53
fertilizing in, 54, 55
laying sod in, 42
mowing in, 49
overseeding in, 73
seeding in, 40
Nosema locustae, 86
Nutsedge, yellow *(Cyperus
    esculentus),* 113

Oenothera spp., 22
Organic fertilizers, 54–55 (table),
    57
Organic matter. *See also* Grass
    clippings
    as fertilizer, 57
    and lawn renovation, 70, 72, 91
    on newly seeded lawn, 42
    on new plants, 23
    and soil preparation, 37, 75
Ornamental grasses, 1, 21
Overfertilizing, 53–54
Overseeding, 29, 72–73
Overwatering, 70

Pachysandra, 16
Parasitic nematodes, 82, 84, 85,
    87, 89
Paspalum dilatatum, 101
Patches, repair of, 73–75
Paths, of grass, 13, 14, 20
Paving stones, 14, 15, 21, 63
Peat moss. *See* Organic matter
Perennial ryegrass. *See* Ryegrass,
    perennial
Pest control, 81–89
Pesticides. *See also names of specific
    pesticides*
    and lawn disease, 90
    and thatch development, 70
Pest-resistant grasses, 72
Pests, 81–89
pH, 36, 70, 93

Planning
amount of lawn, 4
budget considerations, 4, 23,
27, 39, 45
design considerations, 4–12
grass type selection, 25–28
of lawn alternatives, 16, 18–21,
22–23, 67
maintenance considerations,
3–4, 12–16, 22
of meadows and prairies, 22–23
Plantago major, 98
Plantain, 50
broadleaf *(Plantago major),* 98
Planting
of lawns, 25–45
of wildflower meadows and
prairies, 22–23
Plugging tools, 45
Plugs, 39–40, 44–45
Poa
annua, 27, 96, 96
trivalis, 27
Polygonum aviculare, 108
Portulaca oleracea, 110
Powdery mildew, 93
Prairies, 22–23
Problems, diagnosis of, 62–64,
79–81, 91–92. *See also*
Diseases; Pests; Slopes;
Thatch; Weeds
Professional lawn-care assistance,
81, 92
Prostrate knotweed *(Polygonum
aviculare),* 108
Prostrate spurge *(Euphorbia
maculata),* 109
Purslane *(Portulaca oleracea),* 110
Pyrethrin, 84, 87, 88
Pythium blight, 93

Quackgrass *(Agropyron repens),*
111

Rakes, 35, 42, 70
Raking, 56
Red fescue, 20, 26, 32, 69
Red thread, 94
Reel mowers, 50
'Reliant' fine fescue, 90
Removal of lawns, 76, 77
Reseeding, 73–75
Resodding, 73–76
Rollers, 37
Rotary mowers, 49–50
Rotary spreaders, 57
Rotenone, 83
Rough bluegrass *(Poa trivalis),* 27
Rust, 94
Ryegrass, annual, 27, 28, 50
Ryegrass, perennial
and Bermudagrass, 29
description of, 28, 33, 72
mowing of, 49, 50
planting of, 73
zones for, 26

Sabadilla, 85
St. Augustine decline virus, 90
St. Augustine grass
description of, 28, 31
mowing of, 49, 50
planting of, 44, 45
zones for, 26
Sandy soil
corrections for, 36–37
grasses for, 30
Sedums, 21
Seed, buying of, 27, 41
Seed quality, 41
Seeding, 39, 40–42. *See also*
Overseeding; Reseeding
Setaria spp., 103
Shade. *See also* Shade-tolerant
grasses
lawn damage from, 64
planting in, 16, 17, 40

Shade-tolerant grasses, 73
bahiagrass, 29, 49, 50
coarse-bladed grasses, 28
fine fescue, 29, 32, 49, 57, 72
perennial ryegrass, 26, 28, 29,
33, 49, 72, 73
St. Augustine grass, 26, 28, 31,
44, 45, 49, 50
tall fescue, 20, 26, 28, 33, 62,
72
Shape of lawns, 8–12, 68, 69
Sideoats gramma grass, 19, 26
Slice seeders, 73
Slopes. *See also* Grading soil
lawn alternatives for, 3, 16, 67
laying sod on, 44
planning for, 16
Sod. *See also* Sod-forming grasses
budget considerations, 4, 39
description of, 38, 39, 42
laying of, 42–44
making plugs and sprigs
from, 45
resodding, 73–76
Sod-forming grasses, 28
Sod strippers, 76
Sod webworms, 89
Soil
compaction of, 34, 71, 73
drainage of, 36, 62
fertility of, 36–37
grading of, 33–36
healthy, 70, 90–91
pH of, 36, 70, 93
preparation of, 33–37
testing of, 36
watering needs for, 53
Soil types
clay, 30, 36, 37, 53
loamy, 53
sandy, 30, 36, 37, 53
Solarization, 37
Southern U.S.
drought-tolerance in, 53

fertilizing in, 54, 55–57
laying sod in, 42
mowing in, 49
overseeding in, 73
seeding in, 40
Southwestern U.S., nongrass
    home landscapes in, 21
Spills, lawn damage from, 64
"Sports turf," 62
Sprigs, 39–40, 44–45
Sprinkler heads, 51, 52, 53
Spurge, prostrate *(Euphorbia
    maculata),* 109
Square-backed rakes, 35, 42
Stellaria media, 99
Straw, as mulch, 39, 42
String trimmers, 23, 57, 58
Stripe smut, 94
Summer patch, 94

Tall fescue, 20, 26, 28, 33, 49,
    62, 72
Taraxacum officinale, 102
Terraces, 36, 67
Thatch
    description of, 62, 70
    elimination of, 69–70
    grass types prone to, 31
    renovation of lawns with, 73
Thatch rake (cavex), 70
Thyme, 16, 18, 21
Tilling, 37
Tools
    broadcast (drop) seeders,
        41–42
    bulb planters, 7, 23
    core cultivators, 71
    dandelion forks, 95
    dethatchers, 70
    edging tools, 59
    fertilizer spreaders, 57, 72
    grass shears, 57
    hoes, 45

mowers, 48, 49–50
plugging tools, 45
rollers, 37, 42, 43
slice seeders, 73
sod strippers, 76
square-backed rakes, 35, 42
string trimmers, 23, 57, 58
trowels, 23, 43
Top-dressing, 23, 72
Traffic, lawn damage from, 62–64
Traffic-tolerant grasses
    carpetgrass, 30, 49
    perennial ryegrass, 26, 28, 29,
        33, 49, 72, 73
    "sports turf" blend, 62
    tall fescue, 20, 26, 28, 33,
        62, 72
    zoysiagrass, 26, 28, 31, 44,
        45, 49
Trees, maintaining lawns
    around, 14
Trimming, 57–59
Trowels, 23, 43
Turf blocks. *See* Paving stones
Turfgrasses. *See names of specific
    grasses*

USDA hardiness zone map, 115

Verticutters (vertimowers), 70, 73
Vinca, 16

Warm-season grasses. *See also
    names of specific grasses*
    description of, 28, 29–31
    fertilizing of, 55–57
    mowing of, 49
    planting of, 40
Water conservation. *See* Drought-
    tolerant grasses; Watering
Watering, 42, 50–53

Weed-resistant grasses
    (zoysiagrass), 26, 28, 31, 44,
        45, 49
Weeds
    causes of, 95
    control of, 23, 37, 40, 45,
        95–113
    in lawn-grass seed, 27
Weevils (billbugs), 83
Wild garlic *(Allium vineale),* 112
Wildflowers, 17, 22–23

Yarrows *(Achillea* spp.), 22
Yellow nutsedge *(Cyperus
    esculentus),* 113

Zone maps, 26, 115
Zoysiagrass
    description of, 28, 31
    mowing of, 49
    planting of, 44, 45
    zones for, 26

Titles available in the Taylor's Weekend Gardening Guides series:

Organic Pest and Disease Control	$12.95
Safe and Easy Lawn Care	12.95
Window Boxes	12.95
Attracting Birds and Butterflies	12.95
Water Gardens	12.95
Pruning	12.95

At your bookstore or by calling 1-800-225-3362

Prices subject to change without notice